The Leadership Rock
A Journey of a Life of Leadership

Garris Elkins

D1602708

Prophetic Horizons
Jacksonville, OR
United States

The Leadership Rock: A Journey of a Life in Leadership
© 2013 Garris Elkins

Prophetic Horizons
PO Box 509
Jacksonville, OR 97530 USA
info@prophetichorizons.com
www.garriselkins.com

ISBN-10: 0615764029
ISBN-13: 978-0615764023

Cover design by Anna Elkins

Printed in the United States of America.

DEDICATION

I dedicate this book to those of you on a personal life-journey with God. This course of faith is not navigated with finely detailed roadmaps but with the compass of faith that brings us back to true north no matter where we find ourselves. People who bravely follow that compass needle of faith are my heroes. You make life so much more fascinating, and you make God real and personal. I write this book with our common journey in mind.

MY THANKS

I thank the people of the churches I have pastored over the years. You allowed me to work out my calling in your midst. My gratitude for your trust and patience.

I thank leaders—those at the start of their journey, those in the middle, and those on their final steps. I have watched you and learned from your lives.

I thank Jerry Cook for his gracious foreword to this book. His life continues to form and inform mine.

I thank Julie Smith, who said to me, "I saw you writing a book. It was full of wisdom and God experiences."

I thank my daughter, Anna Elkins, for her wonderful editing touch on this our second book together.

I thank my precious wife and best friend, Jan, who lovingly proofreads my life before I have her proofread my manuscript.

And I thank the Lord—you are less complicated than I first thought. It is in your simplicity that you are truly profound. Thank you for unraveling my misconceptions.

CONTENTS

FOREWORD

The church at every level must have the highest quality of leadership. What that high-quality leader looks like has been a point of question and the subject of a myriad of books. The picture has ranged from a leader who simply takes a few Bible courses and then ventures forth, assured of God's call and anointing, to the extreme of the leader patterned after the successful CEO of a large corporation.

Garris Elkins bypasses both of these extremes. He gives us instead the story and observations of an influential missionary and pastoral leader. The story is wrapped around three, recurring refrains:

1. The need to live in the awareness of the presence of God.
2. The reality and necessity of the prophetic, the miraculous, and the immediate word of God.
3. The fact that our calling does not end due to age or circumstances but rather unfolds into the next stage of Jesus' intention and direction.

Practical principles of effective leadership are woven around these themes. They emerge in Garris' own story and reveal to us the passion, thought processes, idea development, and the influence of the presence and voice of

God in his life and ministry. We are given insight into how Garris processed and applied the input of the many significant people in his life.

If you love stories as I do, this book will not only instruct and challenge you, it will delight you. It is not a book of technique or infallible keys. It is the account of a leader living out his calling. In the warmth of that human story, I was encouraged, challenged and, yes, entertained. I found myself underlining many remarks and passages that walked into my heart and spoke life to me.

This is a book that I recommend you not "speed read." Read it slowly, thoughtfully, and repeatedly. It will increase your effectiveness by challenging you to lead sensitively, lead boldly, and lead supernaturally. It will enrich your own life story—whatever chapter is presently being written.

—Jerry Cook
Author of *Love, Acceptance and Forgiveness*

INTRODUCTION

I wrote *The Leadership Rock* because something in the life of Moses caught my attention. During a long battle described in Exodus 17, Moses stood on a mountaintop watching Joshua lead the Israelite troops against their enemy. Moses held his staff above the combat that raged in the valley beneath him. As the battle progressed, Moses realized that his physical limitations would prevent him from keeping his arms raised. The raised staff was giving his army victory. As Moses' fatigue became obvious, Aaron and Hur provided a rock for Moses to sit upon. Moses was wise enough to trust the offer of his friends, sit down, and let them help hold his arms high.

Through his willingness to sit upon the rock, Moses helped bring victory to the army fighting in the valley below. By sitting on the rock, Moses also became a spiritual link: a link to his friends who stood at his side and held up his arms, to victory in the battle that raged before him, to the place of rest the rock provided a weary servant, and to the power of heaven that flowed from above down onto the field of battle.

At times, we try to do this life alone. Solitary lives may appear to work for a while, but then they can become wearisome and dangerous.

I've tried standing on my own, and I've tried sitting on the "rock." I've had far more victory doing the latter. This book shares some of the insights I have learned in over thirty years of ministry.

At some point, we all need to make the choice to sit down and surrender our plan to the Lord's plan. When we assume a posture of rest and surrender, God can accomplish what we cannot do and what only He can do.

If we can keep our lives properly positioned for the spiritual battle before us, we will see supernatural victories that can only be explained because God showed up when we sat down.

1
THE GIFT OF GLADYS

As young church planters, Jan and I knew very little about what it actually meant to plant a church. We had a calling and a measure of faith—and that was all. When we entered the ministry, few resources were available for church planting. I think our early ministry embodied the phrase, "winging it."

When we arrived in Kalispell, Montana, we set up our home, and then I went around town trying to find a place to hold our church services. If we were to do it all over again, we would have started in our home, but that wasn't the model for church planting in our day.

I found a local hotel called The Outlaw Inn that had venue rooms to rent. I secured the Colt 45 room. It seated fifty people, and I set up fifty chairs for our first public service.

I revisited that room a few years ago and wept as I remembered all that God has done in our lives since our awkward start.

The first Sunday felt dismal. We had one visitor, a travelling artist, who arrived midway through the worship time. For the following six weeks, we had only one person attending our meetings. Her name was Gladys. Gladys looked to be in her late 60's. She had lived a rough life. She couldn't drive, so our location at The Outlaw Inn, just across the street from her home, was a good match for her needs.

For those six weeks, we never knew which room we would use for our Sunday church services; the Inn could see we weren't a happening event, so they moved us around to whatever room was available. We would arrive early on Sunday mornings and check in with the front desk to find out our newly assigned room.

Somehow, Gladys found us each time. She liked to have a nip of gin each morning. I think Gladys was a lonely and functioning alcoholic. For those six weeks, she faithfully sat next to my wife, Jan, and our two kids on the front row. The remaining forty-six empty chairs stared back at me while I led worship *a capella* (without instruments) and preached the Word.

At the end of each service, this dear little drunk lady would walk up to me, look up into my face, and with gin-infused breath say, "Thank you, Pastor. I needed to hear that."

I can now appreciate those words of thanks on many different levels. I did not appreciate them at the time. At that time in my life, I had a vision of ministry success that did not include empty chairs and drunk people.

About four weeks into our church planting adventure, I felt like an utter failure. In my naivety, I believed that if you mixed enough faith with a passion to plant a church, one would magically appear. It didn't, and I began to get depressed.

At week four, I asked God why all of this was happening. *Why are only my wife and kids and drunk Gladys showing up?* Then the Lord spoke to me and said, "If you learn to love this one, I will send you more."

Two weeks later, we had enough of the revolving

meeting room issue and decided to move the "church" into our home. Within weeks, a trickle of new faces began to arrive on our doorstep and growth began.

I never saw Gladys after we moved. We lost contact with her. Of all the great things I have had the privilege to learn over my thirty-plus years of ministry, what God taught me through Gladys is one of the most profound. "If you learn to love this one, I will send you more."

I needed to learn how to love. I thought I knew how to love people until God sent me Gladys. God desires to entrust the precious lives of people He loves to shepherds who will love them as well.

2
ROY'S THREE QUESTIONS

Many years ago, when I was a student at Ministries Institute at Faith Center in Eugene, Oregon, I learned a valuable lesson about sermon preparation from my pastor, Roy Hicks, Jr.

Roy was a profound teacher of God's Word and Kingdom. Roy's focus on Kingdom preaching wrecked me for desiring anything less in my own ministry.

In one of our classes Roy said, "There are three questions you need to ask yourself as you prepare to teach God's Word: What is God's heart in the passage? What is the human response? What is the personal application?"

I will never forget Roy's words. Over the years, I have studied the disciplines of sermon preparation, hermeneutics and homiletics, and have benefited from these studies, yet those three questions from Roy have had the strongest influence on my life and teaching ministry.

Once, Roy gave each of us a copy of his sermon notes. I was surprised that it was only one page in length. Embedded in that single page of notes were the answers to his three questions. I still have those notes.

Thirty-five years later, I teach those same three questions to the young men and women who attend our school of ministry in Medford, Oregon. Roy's questions have been so impacting because they have caused me to dig deeper into God's Word beyond just a commentary-level of study.

Roy's questions made me press into the heart of God and apply the Word to my own life as I prepare a message each week.

It has been hard sometimes, but I think this kind of sermon preparation is part of the continuing process of incarnation where the Word becomes flesh in the people of God.

3
THE BIG-SHOT PASTOR

When our kids were in grade school, we pastored a wonderful church on the Oregon Coast for several years. Coastal towns can be great places to live, and our family still looks back on those years with great warmth and affection.

Shortly after we arrived in Newport, we sensed that God was beginning to do something new in the church. The newness was not because Jan and I were now leading the church but because God had decided to do something new.

During one Sunday service, the sanctuary was filled to overflowing, and the worship team led us into a wonderful experience with the presence of the Lord. After I preached the Word, a woman ran up to me and said the words every pastor loves to hear: "Pastor, this is a revival!" I was elated.

On the way home, my then eight-year-old son, David, asked to ride shotgun with dad in the front seat. Jan smiled and sat in the back with our daughter, Anna. As soon as we pulled out of the church parking lot, I began to talk about how powerful the Sunday morning service had been. I talked about everything in great detail. I was on fire.

After I had gone on and on about the morning service, my son—with his sweet, freckled face beaming up at me—tried to ask a question. I cut him off like he was an interruption to The Big Shot Pastor who was recapping all the wonderful things God had done that day.

I drove about a block before looking over to make sure my son had heard my correction. I saw tears in his eyes. The once joyful face of my little buddy was now broken and downcast. His eyes brimmed with tears that began to roll down his face.

I glanced back at the road and realized I had done something terribly wrong. Then David spoke, and I looked toward him. He said, "Dad, I think you need to go away somewhere and find out why you get mad at me sometimes when I try to talk to you." Then he turned his face toward the passenger window.

In that moment, I felt like the largest lineman in the NFL had just gut-punched me. Shame and sorrow came over me like an intense blanket of heat. I felt I had destroyed this precious little guy who had brought me such joy in his eight short years.

It was like time went into slow motion. My foot came off the accelerator and I slowly steered the car to the curb and turned off the motor. I looked over at David. He still had his face turned away from me, pressed against the rain-soaked window. I began talking to the back of his head.

"David, you are more important to me than any church service. I love you and realize that I just hurt you. I am so sorry, son. Please forgive me and give me a chance to not do that again."

David is a man of mercy and wisdom—he has always carried those two gifts. Even from his childhood, and now as a full-grown man, he has extended mercy to those around him. When Jan and I thought we had a situation all figured out, David would add a piece of wisdom that would give us a deeper Kingdom-understanding. Like his biblical namesake, our son had a heart for God.

When I finished speaking my four sentences of repentance, David turned towards me with a gentle smile and said, "I forgive you, Dad."

Those words still ring in my heart to this day and still impact me. We hugged each other. I started the car and we continued our ride home for Sunday lunch. Jan and Anna wisely remained silent in the backseat throughout the entire incident and listened to God at work between a father and his son.

I learned something that day. As wonderful as it can be to witness God at work, that work never takes priority over people. Jesus came and died for people, not great church services or great life accomplishments.

The day I failed miserably as a father is one I will always cherish. When I think of my failure, I can still see my son's smiling face looking up at me, and I can still hear his tender words: "I forgive you, Dad."

One of the most impacting church services I have ever experienced took place in the sanctuary of our parked car on the streets of Newport, Oregon.

4
CHOOSING THE RIGHT ROAD

As a young pastor, I listened a lot. I listened to the many voices of leaders who went before me. There were times in those early years when I would ask a simple question and receive a profound answer. In my first year of pastoring, I asked Jerry Cook one of those simple questions, and his profound answer changed my understanding of leadership. More importantly, his answer radically changed how I viewed God.

For many years, Jerry Cook was the Senior Pastor of East Hill Church in Gresham, Oregon. The church grew to become a large and influential ministry under Jerry's leadership. East Hill's influence wasn't due to its size but to the voice released through its leadership to the greater Church body. Jerry gave us the ability to see a model of leadership in operation that was unique on the Spirit-filled landscape. He taught us to become thinking Pentecostals and not to live in the fear that our thinking would somehow chase the Holy Spirit away.

While sitting in a gathering of pastors, I asked Jerry: "How do you make decisions?" He replied, "When we have a decision to make, we look at all our options. We then choose the one we think sounds the most like God. Then we begin walking down that road."

I asked another question, "What if you made the wrong decision?"

Jerry answered, "God has always been faithful to pick us up from the wrong road and put us on the right road, if our hearts were right."

As Jerry's answers to my questions circled within my mind, I realized I had been given one of those life-truths I would be unpacking for years to come. Jerry not only gave me insight into his leadership style but also into the heart of God.

Jerry's answer deposited several insights into my life:

DECISION-MAKING SHOULD BE COLLEGIAL

Jerry used the word "we" five times to describe how he made decisions that affected the ministry of East Hill. He did not lead from a solitary position. Jerry invited his team to make decisions with him. The "we" word was an invitation that said decision-making can be a shared experience.

DECISION-MAKING INVOLVES RISK

There is an element of risk when we try our best to choose the God-route from among many options. This is what faith is all about. Faith is risky. You risk your reputation. You risk your pride. You risk your self-image. You risk your money and the money of those who entrusted their money to your leadership. Without risk we will never take those first steps of obedience. If there is no risk in our decision-making, faith will be absent from the process.

DECISION-MAKING REPOSITIONS OUR TRUST

Many times, we leaders try to project self-confidence in our decision-making ability when our confidence is better sourced in the Lord. His decision-making is infallible, ours is not. Paul told the church in Corinth, "We have placed our confidence in Him, and he will continue to rescue us" (II Corinthians 1:10). The repositioning of our trust births a confidence that God will be there for us if things go wrong on the journey.

DECISION-MAKING IS A PROCESS THAT REVEALS OUR IMAGE OF GOD

Of all the things I learned that day with Jerry Cook, this one was the most significant. I learned that God is not afraid of my wrong decisions. God was big enough to pick me up off the wrong road and put me down on the right road if my heart was right. If, along the journey, I discovered personal sin, I always had the option of confession and repentance and that made my heart right once again.

This revelation taught me something new and different. I had always thought God let us ride out our innocent wrong decisions to a catastrophic end as some form of punishment or discipline and that was how we learned about his heart. I was wrong.

I could now trust God to always be there for me even when I picked the wrong road—and got a few miles down that wrong road—before realizing my mistake.

These insights have allowed me to grow in the most important element in decision–making: learning about and trusting in the heart of God.

5
CHALLENGED AUTHORITY

I'd like to share another Jerry Cook story that was pivotal to my leadership growth.

In the first few months of pastoring, I was sitting around a table with five other young and inexperienced pastors. We were in a small meeting room at Montana State University in Billings, Montana. Seated with us was Jerry Cook, author of the book, *Love, Acceptance and Forgiveness.* Jerry was the guest speaker that weekend at Faith Chapel in Billings, and he was also scheduled to speak with our group of pastors.

As Jerry spoke, I could see that he had a powerful command of words and body language. He was also able to communicate the deeper truths about God with great humility.

Jerry gave us a piece of wisdom that day that has stuck with me all these years. He said, "Your authority will never be established until it is challenged." That sentence seemed to freeze-dry itself in midair. I really didn't know what it meant because I was so young in leadership at the time, but I was smart enough to write it down and commit it to memory.

Dealing with anyone who challenges authority is not an excuse for leaders to "power up" and bear down in order to reassert their authority. Rather, it is an opportunity for leaders to evaluate their personal responses to the challenge and hopefully move into new dimensions of their calling.

When our authority is challenged, we have a chance to learn a few things:

1. We can learn what our perceived authority is really based on. If it is a God-given authority, it will still be there after all the messes made during the challenge are cleaned up.

2. We can learn that our God-given authority does not need defending. God-given authority is established by God and empowered by His Spirit. A smart leader simply walks in authority and holds it with an opened hand. God does the establishing part. We never have to grasp our authority to make it secure.

3. We can learn that how we respond when our authority is challenged carries a far greater impact on those who watch our response than the challenge itself. When leaders get insecure, we can say and do very foolish and regretful things as we respond to the challenge. People get hurt by insecure leaders.

4. We can learn that sometimes we are dead wrong in how we moved in our God-given authority, and we *needed* to be challenged. It is never comfortable to be corrected. Each time this happens, a wise leader will ask God,

"What in this challenge is you? What are you wanting to say to me?" There is always something to take away that can make us a better leader.

Whether you lead in the business world, the church, or at home, somewhere in that process of leadership, you will face a challenge. Expect it, but don't live in fear of it. God uses authority—and the challenge to it—as one of many tools to advance His Kingdom. He uses the challenge to a leader's authority to advance the leader. If you are in a season where you are being challenged, God has good things planned for you. Rest in Him. Trust Him. Love the challenger, and then watch your authority become established because of the challenge.

6
A HUNDRED-DOLLAR CRY

In 1981, when Jan and I journeyed to Montana with our children to plant our first church, we had no idea what we were doing. We simply had a word from God and decided to act upon that word in faith.

After a few months went by, my parents came for a visit. Mom and dad grew up living the rough and scrabble life of working-class America during the Great Depression. They knew what tough times felt like. They could see that we were struggling.

It's strange how we can be "all grown up" as adults and find ourselves responding to our parents like we are still twelve-year-old kids. Most of the time, we can manage to hold this child-in-an-adult-body response inside, but sometimes it comes out. During my parents' visit, my inner twelve-year-old spoke out a few times in frustration.

When mom and dad visited, less than ten people—including our family—attended our church. To me it felt like I was being put on display as a pastoral failure. When my parents visited, I seemed to let more emotions out. I felt afraid, alone, and worried about my first attempt at public ministry.

The day mom and dad departed, Jan and I stood on our porch and waved goodbye as their Oldsmobile pulled out of our driveway and disappeared down our dusty Montana road. I felt the sorrow of saying goodbye to two people who brought me such a sense of security.

I went back into the house and sat at my desk which was located in the corner of our bedroom. When I picked up my Bible, I found a hundred-dollar bill lying underneath. I knew my parents had left the money for us. We were living from one meager offering to the next. As I held that bill in my hand, I broke down and began to cry like a baby. All the emotions I had carried for months began to puddle on my desktop.

A single act of unsolicited love can be powerful. That hundred-dollar bill had no note or condition attached to it. The bill just sat there, but it spoke deeply to me. It said, "We love you, son, God is in this. Don't give up."

I have come to see these acts of love—acts of love without words or notes attached to them—as some of the most powerful. They are powerful because they allow the recipient to attach their personal emotion and experience to them.

That day, as I looked out from my desk across the Montana landscape, I felt a deeper love and appreciation for my parents. They gave me a gift of love that helped me continue to walk deeper on my journey of faith without giving up. I knew that through my parents' act of unsolicited love, God was saying to me, "I love you, Garris. I am with you in this. Don't give up."

7

LOVERS AND HISTORIANS

Before Jan and I planted our first church, our pastor, Roy Hicks Jr., called us into his office for an appointment to solidify some final details before we were deployed. During our conversation, Roy asked us if we were ready to pastor and if we understood what it meant.

We ignorantly and innocently responded, "Yes!"

Roy then said something that has followed us for the last several decades as we have ministered in the United States and overseas. Roy said, "When you go to plant the church, go there and be a lover of the people and a student of their history."

Roy did not send us away with a results-oriented assignment. He sent us away with a wisdom that has followed church planters for the last 2,000 years. We honestly had no idea how to plant a church, but to be "lovers and historians" made sense to us—we could do that.

When we didn't know what to do in any given assignment, loving people became a great default. When we couldn't figure out why people responded in a negative way to our acts of love, a study of their personal history helped us see them in a different light—a merciful light.

When we love people just where they are, and when we know their personal history, a couple of things happen. Loving people will always bring a blessing, not only to the one being loved, but also to the one who gives the love. Our love may be rejected, but when we choose to love, we are tapping into the very heart of God, and that heart will sustain us even when our best attempts to love and lead others seem to be failing.

When we study the history of any group of people, we begin to see their lives from the viewpoint of God's mercy. History helps us understand that some of the painful and hurtful things people do to us are not always personal, and we should not take them personally. Negative responses to our acts of love are how people have made their painful history work for them. We simply get in the way of their reaction and take a hit.

In each new season of life you enter, take a moment and commit yourself to be a lover and a historian of those you are called to lead. The acts of love you release, and the knowledge of the history you gain, will create a buffer between you and the strident seasons that ministry will inevitably bring your way. Loving people amidst their broken history is a powerful testimony of God's love.

8
MARGIN TIME

Several years ago, I realized that if I was going to finish well I would need to invest in things that helped me to go deeper in my intimacy with God. In a lifetime of ministry, external demands had started taking over my calendar and daily schedule. I wanted to make an adjustment, but I did not know how.

As I processed this with the Lord, I knew He wanted me to create a space somewhere in my week where duty wasn't present. God wanted me to create a place where I did not study or have to respond to the needs of others. This time would be one apart from my daily devotional time with God or studying for sermons. This time would resemble a walk with God in the coolness of Eden's evening.

While I was first processing this, our church was having a weekly Wednesday night service. I would normally go into the office at nine a.m. each Wednesday and stay through the evening. It made for a long day.

I remember distinctly the Lord saying, "Give me Wednesday morning." I began to ask Him what that would look like.

Our home in Southern Oregon is nestled in a small historic community surrounded by hiking trails. I decided to spend my time with God on those trails each Wednesday morning.

When I made the decision, my first Wednesday time was still a week away, so I had time to think about what those mornings might look like.

This time would be a spiritual cartilage between myself and the demands of my life. No tasks allowed; God wanted me to give Him a chunk of time solely devoted to Him.

At first I thought I should bring my Bible along on these hikes. He said no. Then I thought I should go up on the mountaintop and have formal devotions with Him. He said no. With each suggestion I brought to Him to show I would be faithfully involved in some task, He said no. He wanted nothing from me but my presence. This was not to be a "productive" place.

When that first Wednesday morning rolled around, I put on my hiking boots and set out for the trails. I distinctly remember crossing the threshold between the city and the forest. When I did, I said, "I am all yours, God." I have been saying those same words every week for the last ten years. This weekly hike with God has been one of the most significant times for God to develop me as a person and as a pastor. I hike year round in the rain, snow, and sun.

One personal impact from these Wednesday hikes is the creativity they release. An uncluttered mind is free to dream and pray for those things Paul described in Ephesians 3:20 that are "beyond." Things beyond all that we would ever dare to ask or think or imagine are called into our reality in these times. My own ministry of writing got its birthing push on the trails above Jacksonville, Oregon on my weekly hikes.

I have come to call this Wednesday hike my "margin time." Margin time is that space we give to God that is not invaded with anything. This place is where He can communicate with us while we are untethered to any form of duty or productivity. This dedicated time becomes a creative garden where the seeds of heaven are planted in our lives. For me, this margin time has been my walk in the forest. For others it is getting on a motorcycle, or riding a bike, or sitting in a favorite chair. The way you spend this time is between you and God.

Recently, I told a group of pastors that some of the best books are being written by leaders after they experience burnout or failure. Some of the books, written before the burnout, were all about cramming more and more "good" things into your life to get the most return for your investment in ministry. The books written by leaders after their personal crisis ask us instead to pursue places that resemble a spiritual mountain trail where the stress of life and ministry does not have a voice.

Like a human knee without cartilage, our lives can be so bone-on-bone that we end up becoming crippled. It is the cartilage—that space between the bones—that allows us to move forward. Each leader needs to create a place of margin time where the presence of God acts as a cushion between the urgencies of life and our long-term effectiveness. God is already present in your margin time. He is waiting there to be discovered.

It is Sunday as I write this, and I am already looking forward to the upcoming Wednesday morning in the woods. God is already there waiting for me.

9

SITTING ON THE LEADERSHIP ROCK

Exodus 17 tells of a battle. Moses stood on a mountaintop holding up his staff to heaven while Joshua and the troops fought the Amalekites in the valley below. If Moses held his staff up above his head the troops would win, but if he dropped his hands they would lose.

Joshua and the Israelites were fighting the Amalekites, the descendants of Esau. Esau was the man who sold his birthright for a bowl of stew. He was an opportunist whose life was defined by meeting his pressing needs in the moment and thereby forfeiting his future destiny.

The Amalekites were a nation of nomadic herders who traveled from one patch of green grass to another in order to feed their flocks. In Deuteronomy the Exodus 17 battle is retold with the addition that the Amalekites would attack the rear of a column of people to take down the weak and weary. They were opportunists like their ancestor, Esau. Their tactics resembled those of a pack of wolves.

On the day of the battle, Moses told Joshua to fight the Amalekites while he raised his staff on the mountain. This staff had played an important role in the nation of Israel. The people knew it represented God's power and authority. Moses ascended the mountain, taking Aaron and Hur with him.

The battle plan Moses laid out would make some people uncomfortable. The practically minded would say, "All hands on deck, Moses. We need everyone in the battle. Pray later, it's time to fight." The problem with God's battle plans is that they are not guaranteed to be practical. Some of the most important ingredients in God's plan for victory will not make sense to a natural way of thinking.

If we allow ourselves to be held hostage to only practical solutions for spiritual challenges, we will shut the door to the very steps of faith that are required of us in order to live a supernatural life and experience supernatural breakthrough. The battle Joshua fought that day was determined more by what happened on the mountaintop in prayer than by what took place on the actual battlefield.

As long as Moses held up the staff in his hand, the Israelites had the advantage. But whenever he dropped his hand, the Amalekites gained the advantage. Moses' arms soon became so tired he could no longer hold them up. So Aaron and Hur found a stone for him to sit on. Then they stood on each side of Moses, holding up his hands. So his hands held steady until sunset. As a result, Joshua overwhelmed the army of Amalek in battle (Exodus 17: 11-13).

What caught my attention in this passage was the use of the stone. When Moses went up on the mountain, I am sure he had no thought about sitting on a rock. He saw himself standing tall with the staff held high above his head. That is a dramatic posture but one that is not possible to hold long term.

As the battle progressed, it became obvious that the original plan was not going to work. Each time Moses got tired and dropped his hands, some of his men died. Hands up and people lived. Aaron and Hur saw what was taking place. They looked around for something for Moses to sit on and provided him with a rock.

Aaron and Hur brought the rock because they saw that Moses was focused on the life-and-death task of holding up his staff. One of Moses' greatest leadership acts would be his willingness to sit on the rock that others had provided.

Two principles for life emerge in this text. First, those who lead in any capacity need to be willing to assume a posture of ministry that was unplanned but which allows them to do what God has called them to do without burning out before the victory comes. Plans change, and leaders must be willing to adapt.

Victory always comes from a place of rest. Rest is a place of trust. That is the nature of living in God's grace and favor. The reality is that somewhere in the battle we may realize we need a seat of rest if we are going to finish well.

The second reality is our posture of life. We are called to work from a place of rest. When we live alongside each other, it is easier for us to access each other's arms and hold each other up for long periods of time. This only works if we are seated in a place of rest that gives people access to our life.

If Aaron and Hur had stood with Moses and held his arms with the staff, it would have looked dramatic, but their posture would not have lasted long term. All three men would have grown weary and dropped their arms and the staff. The result would have been fatigue and defeat.

None of us can stand up in our own strength for long. The most strategic battles in life are fought from a place of rest. We all need to learn when to sit down and when to let others help us instead of doing life in our own strength.

I am beginning to think that one of the greatest lessons in life is learning when to sit down, and one of the greatest assignments in a friendship is knowing how to find a rock for our friends to sit on.

10
TRUSTING IN BROKEN NETS

Early one morning, I was reading through the Book of Habakkuk. Like all of the books written by the prophets, context and audience are important, and yet, as I was reading, some verses stood out and spoke to me.

I began to import some of those Scriptures into my morning prayers. As I prayed, God began to ask me some questions.

> Then they will worship their nets and burn incense in front of them. These nets are the gods who have made us rich! (Habakkuk 1:16).

I thought of the beautiful painting that hangs above my office desk. The painting is a watercolor depicting the disciples hauling in a net full of fish. The net is breaking and the disciples are looking up to heaven from their boat that is being tossed about on the raging waves of a storm. Their physical posture is focused upward in a petition for God to help them.

There are times when I feel like some of my nets are

breaking. I feel like I am in the painting looking to heaven for help.

As I read Habakkuk the first God-question came: "Has your model of ministry become an idol to you?" Many times I think I really have things figured out. When the fruit of success is being hauled in, it is all too easy to begin thinking we really know what we are talking about. When the model of ministry—our current net—begins to rip, where do we look for help? Do we begin looking for another model of ministry to replace the old one, or do we look to God? I want to become one of the disciples in the boat in the painting who looks up, not around.

> How foolish to trust in your own creation—a god that can't even talk! (Habakkuk 2:18b).

I have been doing pastoral ministry for a long time. It is easy to slip into thinking that whatever good happens is somehow the result of the labor of my hands. While God wants us to be faithful, He is constantly reminding me that eternal things are only built by His hands; we partner with Him, but He alone builds. He builds the Church while we keep the environment within His construction project healthy and honest.

The question I heard attached to this verse was, "What are you trusting in, Garris?"

Am I trusting in what I have promoted in myself, my assignment, and calling, or am I trusting in those things that don't require my promotion because what God has done will bear its own witness? It is too easy to slip into self-promotion when we want to see something happen. Idols get carved in our insecure seasons and they begin to look like us.

> In this time of our deep need, help us again as you did in years gone by (Habakkuk 3:2).

Many of us who lead and serve in the Church, if we were brutally honest, would say, "This is a time of deep personal need. God come and show me again your manifest presence and your power—save me again!" This is where I have been parked lately. As a pastor, I feel my own needs and pain, but I also carry—and sometimes in a wrong way—the struggles of those I have been called to shepherd.

Then the questions for this verse came: "Do you want it your way or my way? Is your need deep enough now that there is nothing left of your abilities to come to the rescue? Do you still believe I have something to do in you that is beyond all you could ask or hope for?"

11
CROSSING THRESHOLDS

One of the most stressful things I have ever done was to be an entry man on a SWAT team. Entry men are the first members of the team to breach a door and cross the threshold of a house to gain entrance. We never knew what was waiting for us on the other side of the door.

Before making entry, the team would gather around the doorstep of the house and then kick in the door. My fellow entry man was taller than me, so he went high and I went low. If there was going to be any altercation, it would be in those moments right after the splintered doorframe flew across the room and five, heavily armed SWAT team members entered the house to make an arrest.

How you crossed the threshold determined if you lived or died. It is a serious business and is literally a science in the world of police tactics.

Our goal was never to get to the other side and bring death. Our desire was that, through superior tactics, whatever we encountered on the other side would yield to our presence and life would be spared.

It has been many years since I was a member of a SWAT team. At this age, I would get myself in trouble if I tried to do what my youthful strength allowed back then.

Over the years, I have come to realize that all of life is filled with thresholds that can produce life or death, depending on how we prepare to make the crossing.

Everyday we cross thresholds in life. A marriage matures by crossing the threshold of forgiveness. Friends cross a threshold when they decide to risk sharing their deepest pain with each other. Parents cross a threshold when they release a child to become an adult. How we navigate these relational barriers is important. In each crossing, we want to bring life—not death—to those we greet on the other side. I have not been perfect in crossing my thresholds, but it has been a life goal of mine to try to cross them well.

Here are my daily thresholds:

THE THRESHOLD OF AWAKENING

As each of us awake in the morning, our first conscious thoughts are powerful and can direct the course of our day. It is too easy to wake up and let a stressful calendar or a scheduled meeting with a difficult person set our day's tone. I want the first thought in my mind to simply be, "Thank you, Jesus." I thank Him simply because I am alive in Him— again. This first threshold is crossed with thankfulness.

THE THRESHOLD OF FIRST WORDS

I am usually up before my wife, Jan. As I exit the bathroom in the darkness, I sometimes hear her rustle in bed. I let her choose to respond first so as not to awaken her. When she hears me walking back into the bedroom, she will usually say, "Good morning." My first words to my wife in the darkness are, "Good morning, I love you." This threshold is crossed with tender recognition.

THE THRESHOLD OF A NEW DAY

I set our coffee maker up before I go to bed at night. I like this arrangement because, in the morning, all I have to do is hit the "brew" button on my way through the kitchen en route to my chair where I will have my morning devotions. When I arrive in the living room, I kneel at my chair and say the same thing each day, "This is the day the Lord has made, and I will rejoice and be glad in it." I add a few more lines to this prayer, but these words link my day to rejoicing. I cross this threshold by choosing to have an attitude of joy.

THE THRESHOLD OF COMMUNION

A few years ago, Jan and I began taking communion together each day. It has been the most profound devotional time for us as a couple. It only takes a few minutes. We use unleavened bread and pour some port wine into a special chalice and remember God together. Our time of communion is sometimes filled with confession and repentance. We always cross over by praying for our kids and, almost without fail, the Church. This threshold is crossed as we choose to remember the Lord together.

THE THRESHOLD OF WORK

Each day, as I turn onto Roberts Road and see our church facility a few blocks away, I ask God to pour out His Spirit upon me and our staff and the church so that we can accomplish His plan for the day. What God wants to do each day can only be accomplished in His wisdom and power. This threshold is crossed when I remain dependent on God.

THE THRESHOLD OF RETURNING HOME

A block or two before I arrive home, I do a quick review of my day and see what I need to unload on God before I get home and unload on Jan. Sometimes this is a prayer of repentance, and other times it is simply choosing to be thankful for the person and home to which I am returning. This threshold is crossed by not forgetting that I have been given the gift of returning.

THE THRESHOLD OF THE EVENING

The Bible says not to let the sun go down on our anger. For most of the year, there are several hours between the setting of the sun and when we finally go to bed. Hours of unresolved anger and bitterness can ruin an evening with a family. Crossing this threshold means engaging how we really feel and choosing to turn off the TV and computers and getting things right so that joy, not sorrow, is the atmosphere of our home.

THE THRESHOLD OF BEDTIME

Crossing this threshold, I kneel each night at our bed and ask God to speak to Jan and me in our dreams and to bless our sleep. This time is often when we discover if we have been honest with each other throughout the day. Years ago, I made a commitment that each night, when the lights go out and we got into bed, I would say to Jan, "Good night, I love you." If I have any difficulty saying those words to Jan, the light comes back on and we deal with whatever it is that is robbing us of peace. Crossing this threshold each night requires uttering my commitment and being willing to deal with my pride.

Crossing thresholds is something we each do multiple times every day. Many times we find ourselves allowing our emotions or the painful events from our day to direct these crossings. We have the power of choice. We can choose to do these crossings differently and arrive on the other side healthy, alive, and more in love with each other.

12

END WITH THE BEGINNING IN MIND

In the late 1980's and early 1990's, many pastors in America hung out in the business section of their local bookstores. In those aisles stuffed with business knowledge were books that drew their titles from subjects like swimming with sharks, searching for excellence, creating wealth, and one-minute approaches to business, health, and everything else. All the titles were verb-oriented. We all wanted to get things moving.

Stephen Covey's book, *The Seven Habits of Highly Effective People,* was especially popular. Covey helped guide people into more productive lives. Most of us read the book and implemented its concepts into our personal lives and ministries. Covey's points made sense. For many years, these principles served us well and still do in some circumstances.

There are a lot of life-plan programs out there. Covey is now one among many. What I have come to realize about life-plans is that they work long term if they are built upon a word from God. The development of a plan must follow a word of revelation that is only available from God by His Spirit. These words are not found in the business section of a bookstore. If the plan is to work, it must rest on revelation. In the middle of the night, when doubt and fear come visiting, it will be the word of the Lord—not a plan—that will bring us comfort.

One of Covey's classic lines was, "Begin with the end in mind." He asked us to imagine the finished product before we began to create a plan to make our vision a reality. With that finished product in mind, we would then return to the present moment and create and define measurable steps for a process that would lead us to the realization of our desired goal.

While Covey was right about developing a plan, there is something going on in my heart that is shifting the process around. Many of us are looking for a jump-start to reignite our vision and calling. We want a plan to finish well.

To finish well requires that we make adjustments now for a strong finish later. This way of planning for a strong finish has us start with the beginning, not the end, in mind. Some of us will need to recapture our beginning if we are going to experience fruitfulness in our ending.

Several years ago, I was in Indianapolis for a training event and had the pleasure of having lunch with Dr. Bob Logan. Bob is well known in church circles for developing leadership training and church planting materials that are considered some of the best around.

During one of the lunch breaks, I sat at a table with Bob and several others. As the lunch conversation progressed, I asked, "Bob, what advice do you give to individuals or organizations who have plateaued or are in decline? How do you help them get moving again?"

I asked this knowing that Bob is very gifted in evaluating the effectiveness of individuals and corporations, and people use his advice with great confidence.

Bob's answer was interesting. He said, "The first thing I

ask is this, 'What was your original vision.'" He went on to say most leaders are able to recite their vision in great detail. Bob would then ask a set of questions to determine if the leaders were still functioning in their original vision. Within plateaued or declining corporations and ministries there was a common reality: each one had stopped doing the very thing that brought them success in the first place. They had ceased doing their original vision.

Bob then shared a powerful truth with me, "Each time someone rediscovered their original vision and began to do it once again, in each case, without exception, they began to move forward and grow."

I sat there wonderfully stunned by what I just heard. The lunch conversation continued to move around the table, but I was still processing the words, "in each case, without exception."

When God does an original work in our lives, there is more going on than something new and refreshing. In these times, foundations are being built and vision is being cast. Those first few years are the time when He develops and defines the spiritual DNA structure that will carry us into the future towards a fruitful end. Most of the decisions I make today are sourced in the original truth and wisdom I learned in my first few years of ministry.

The times of my wife's and my personal renewal and redirection have always taken place when we rediscovered and revisited our original DNA. Once we reengaged those origins, we began to experience new traction and movement.

At this point in our lives, Jan and I are living out those basic truths in deeper and wider applications that many years of walking with Jesus can bring. Our vision may be deeper and wider now, but it is all based on the original truths revealed to us in those early years.

What did God give you as a vision or direction when you first began your journey of faith? Are you doing that now? If not, chances are you have either plateaued or are in decline. You might be scrambling around for a new word or some fresh concept to grasp. Maybe your answer for a jump-start is already in your life and simply needs to be revisited, redefined, and reengaged. Go back to the beginning and take a new look at that first word, embrace its truth, and new life will begin to flow once again.

13
THIS GOOD NEWS

And God chose me to be a preacher, an apostle, and a
teacher of this Good News. — II Timothy 1:11

There is a sense of urgency in both of the letters Paul wrote
to his spiritual son, Timothy. Paul speaks as a concerned
father wanting his son to stir up the deposit God had placed
in his life.

Preaching the Word was one of the most important
things Paul reminded Timothy to do. Verse eleven is
couched between two subjects: Paul telling Timothy to not
be ashamed of the Gospel and Paul stating that the reason
for his imprisonment was for preaching the Gospel.

Paul's preaching about Christ was a life-priority to him,
as it should be to each believer—not just to those who stand
behind a pulpit each week.

Preaching the message of the Good News got Paul in
trouble in many of the places he traveled. His jeopardy did
not come from teaching on the structure of the Church or
how to deliver a prophetic word. The Good News Paul

preached was a volatile subject about salvation in Christ alone that turned his contemporary world upside down.

I am seeking a simpler order for the priorities of my calling as a follower of Jesus Christ. I don't want to over-complicate what God wants to do in and through me. It has become too easy for me to seek a gift-based definition for what I do at the expense of simply declaring the message of Christ on a daily basis.

I have to be careful not to retreat into my equipping gifts instead of preaching and declaring Jesus. Maybe the equipping ministry of the various gifts given to the Church could simply be the recognition of how each of us preaches the Good News? Some in the Church are apostolic preachers of the Good News. Others are evangelistic preachers of the Good News. Still others can be either a prophet or a teacher or a pastor, but all preach the Good News while they function in their unique and defined calling.

In the Church, many of us have wanted our ministry to become so defined that we may have moved beyond the simple and pure devotion to Jesus to which we were originally called. Such devotion is birthed out of our understanding of the Good News.

Paul defined his personal ministry in this order: preacher, apostle, and teacher. All three of these definitions had added to them the words, "of this Good News." Paul was a *preacher* of this Good News, an *apostle* of this Good News and a *teacher* of this Good News. All that he was found its source in proclaiming "this Good News."

We all could learn from Paul's instruction to Timothy. Paul had to remind Timothy what the order of his ministry was: preacher, apostle, and teacher. No matter which of the ministry descriptions Timothy would function within at any given time, Paul desired this definition to describe what Timothy did in his ministry: "this Good News."

Every follower of Christ is called to be a preacher

of "this Good News." From within these believers—the Church—who are positioned around the world in every culture, there will emerge bands of apostles, prophets, evangelists, pastors, and teachers who will begin to equip the Church to do the work of the ministry. That work of ministry will always include the sharing of "this Good News" no matter what other ministry description a person carries.

14

WALKING IN CIRCLES AND THANKING JESUS

When I was a young pastor in training, I was part of a church called Faith Center in Eugene, Oregon. This wonderful church took a step of faith with me and let me try my hand at counseling people.

I was so green, and yet there I was—in an office sitting across a desk from people who were pouring out their hearts to me. I would nod like I understood what they were experiencing and then try to offer some God-advice.

The temporary office I used was available at certain hours of the day. It was a nondescript room without a name on the door. One day, I was sitting in the desk chair and looking out the window while waiting for my next appointment. The office window looked out onto a small patio surrounded by hedges. The patio was only accessible from the private office of the senior pastor of our church, Roy Hicks, Jr., and it wasn't visible from any other window.

As I stared out the window, I noticed Roy step out of his office and walk onto the patio. Roy was one of those rare leaders who carried an immense presence of authority. He was highly respected in our church movement and by many others across the globe.

Roy didn't look happy. His face showed concern and maybe a bit of anger. And then Roy began to walk in circles. The patio was small, so the circles were, too. As Roy began to walk in tight, little circles, I heard him repeating over and over again, "Thank you, Jesus. Thank you, Jesus. Thank you, Jesus." This went on for a few moments then he went back into his office.

Over my years of leading in the Church, I have recalled, on numerous occasions, what Roy demonstrated to me that day. I learned that he carried whatever was troubling him out onto the patio and began to search for a thankful heart in the midst of a difficult moment. This life-lesson said to me, "When nothing makes sense, start thanking Jesus because a thankful heart will become an understanding heart." I think the limiting real estate of that small patio was also part of another life-lesson: "Stay put and don't move on until your heart changes."

I have learned that this kind of understanding doesn't mean we will understand why people do what they do to upset us in the first place. It simply means that each hassle and problem of life is an opportunity to focus more deeply on the One who loves us, and that focus is our reason for thanksgiving.

If you see me walking in tight little circles someday while mumbling to myself, you will know what I'm up to.

Thanks, Roy.

15

WHAT OTHERS THINK ABOUT US

People will choose to see leaders in many different lights. I've had some people love and respect me and other people make unkind comments about me on their way out the door. I am learning that I cannot take things personally.

I had the honor of speaking at a national conference in Los Angeles. The person who introduced me is one of the most respected and recognizable faces in the Church, both in the United States and around the world. When I was introduced, this person said some very honoring things about my life and ministry. I was overwhelmed with the favor that had been extended to me.

That same week, a woman left our church because she didn't like me. She came to her conclusion without talking with me and decided I was a major problem in her life. Her anger and dishonor fell on me like a load of mud.

Some people may love you, and others may not like you at all. This is not just a problem for pastors; all people will encounter these differences if they live long enough. What really matters in life is what *God* thinks of us. He described

His children as *loved, forgiven,* and *accepted.* God chooses to see us this way even when all our warts, blemishes, and failures are fully visible to Him. He knows everything about His children, and He still loves us.

When I was introduced at the conference in Los Angeles, my pride kicked in, and I immediately had to park the kind words spoken about me at the feet of Jesus. When the woman left our church, I had to park her angry words at the feet of Jesus also. When we lay them at His feet, Jesus can touch the words spoken about us—the good and the bad—and transform them into a healthy influence in our lives.

When we give God possession of what others think about us, He can grow us past the personal definitions others have given us so that we can begin to live our lives more like the person He has already declared us to be in His Son, Jesus Christ.

16

CROSSING SPIRITUAL FRONTIERS

Everyone crosses spiritual frontiers at one time or another. People leave old seasons of life and enter into new ones. It is important to understand what takes place in these passages.

One of the most profound crossings ever made was when the nation of Israel walked across the dry riverbed of the Jordan River under the leadership of Joshua. More than one million people camped at the water's edge waiting for the word of the Lord to part the water. First, God would need to speak to Joshua and let him know what this passage would entail:

> After the death of Moses the Lord's servant, the Lord spoke to Joshua son of Nun, Moses' assistant. He said, "Moses my servant is dead. Therefore, the time has come for you to lead these people, the Israelites, across the Jordan River into the land I am giving them. I promise you what I promised Moses: 'Wherever you set foot, you will be on land I have given you—from the Negev wilderness in the south to the Lebanon mountains in the north, from the Euphrates River in the east to the Mediterranean Sea in the west, including all the land of

the Hittites.' No one will be able to stand against you as long as you live. For I will be with you as I was with Moses. I will not fail you or abandon you. Be strong and courageous, for you are the one who will lead these people to possess all the land I swore to their ancestors I would give them. Be strong and very courageous. Be careful to obey all the instructions Moses gave you. Do not deviate from them, turning either to the right or to the left. Then you will be successful in everything you do. Study this Book of Instruction continually. Meditate on it day and night so you will be sure to obey everything written in it. Only then will you prosper and succeed in all you do. This is my command—be strong and courageous! Do not be afraid or discouraged. For the Lord your God is with you wherever you go" (Joshua 1:1-9).

Because of the Israelites' previous doubt, they had spent many years wandering in the wilderness until a generation of disbelief died off. Joshua and the nation of Israel wanted to get it right this time. Joshua would come to realize several important truths about crossing spiritual frontiers:

EACH CROSSING WILL BE DIRECTED BY A WORD FROM GOD

The Lord spoke to Joshua

Joshua was told to walk anywhere within the land God had defined. Wherever Joshua chose to step would be his, within the boundary of the promise. He was a man living under the direction of God's revelation.

Every circumstance and relationship we enter into has a word from the Lord assigned to it that will direct how it will develop. It is wise to discover these words before we begin our journey.

Joshua obeyed the word of the Lord. He didn't deviate to the right or to the left. He stayed true to the word of the Lord, and the Lord stayed true to the promise He made to Joshua and the nation of Israel.

Each Crossing Will Redefine the Nature of Our Calling

The time has come for you to lead these people

Moses was dead. A transition in national leadership had taken place. Joshua was now the leader of Israel. The steps of the nation would follow the steps of their new leader. Obedience to the call transformed Joshua, revealing more of what God saw in him, had planned for him, and wanted to do through him.

Like a master sculptor, God chisels us with each step of faith we take. Under the hand of the Master, we begin to resemble the person we already are in Christ at the right hand of the Father.

Each Crossing Will Carry a Promise into a New Generation

I promise you what I promised Moses

We each carry a promise. When we die, that promise does not die with us—it lives on. The promises of God survive through the pain of divorce or the fears associated with financial collapse. Promise lives on through all kinds of personal failure. A promise from God is birthed in eternity high above the powers of death and the finality of time.

When Joshua was about to lead Israel through the visible frontier of the Jordan River at flood stage, he was carrying the promise of a past generation: "I promise you what I promised Moses." Joshua carried that promise forward past the failed first attempt to enter the Promise Land.

Each of us can step in faith into the promise of God,

despite the failures of our past or the failures of others. While we must be faithful and step forward into the Promise, God is the One Who will be faithful to ensure its final delivery.

EACH CROSSING WILL BRING A REMINDER OF GOD'S FAITHFULNESS

I will not fail you or abandon you

We never do what God calls us to do alone. He is always present with us in each moment of the passage. When Joshua called the people forward to cross the Jordan, that move appeared to be foolish. The decision to cross the Jordon River at flood stage would ride on the shoulders of this new leader. That moment of decision was a fearful and stressful one, but God assured Joshua that He would not fail or abandon him.

As a pastor, a father, a brother, and a friend, I have at times lived under fear and isolation, hoping that God would be there for me. We all struggle with this from time to time. Fear in the present is often tied to our assumption of future rejection and abandonment.

Fear of abandonment is experienced everywhere. Spouses have abandoned their vows of marriage and left their mate for someone else. Children have abandoned their parents, and parents have abandoned their children. Employers have abandoned faithful employees for greater profit. In those times, God reminds us—as He reminded Joshua—of His covenant of unfailing love promising He will never leave us alone in the journey.

There is a way out of the prison of abandonment; we forgive and bless our way across this spiritual frontier. Jesus chose to forgive His tormentors amidst the pain of His crucifixion. He told us to bless our enemies even as they wage war against us. When we do this, our future will be defined by the heart of God, not the fear of what can happen to us as the result of human brokenness.

EACH CROSSING WILL TEST OUR CURRENT LEVEL OF STRENGTH AND COURAGE

Be strong and courageous

Three times in the first verses of Joshua 1 the Lord tells Joshua, "Be strong and courageous." Why would God say this to Joshua three times? Because Joshua, the great warrior-leader, would experience both weakness and fear as he faced the prospect of crossing the swollen Jordan River and the enemies beyond it.

Fear and discouragement have faced the people of God in the past, and they will have to be addressed by each of us now and in our emerging future. A repeated theme in Paul's ministry was his strengthening and encouraging of the churches. He strengthened and encouraged these churches because they were feeling weak and discouraged when he arrived in their midst.

Today, choose to believe God is taking you into a new future amidst all the pain and obstacles that are now standing between you and what He has promised. God is your passage-maker, and He will never leave you alone in the crossing you are about to make.

17

THE ISSUES ARE NOT THE ISSUE

I sent an email that was prophetic in nature to a friend of mine. He was facing a situation where he needed encouragement and direction. The obvious issue was not what he really needed to navigate. Something deeper was at work.

This leader was called upon to deal with issues that impacted a wide and diverse audience. I felt the Lord was saying to this person: "the issues are not the issue." It sounded simplistic, because we understand that the human issues we face each day are not always the God-issues we need to discover. These God-issues are buried deep beneath our history, our preferences, and our current culture. It is in the discovery of these God-issues that we find peace and resolution which then affects the surface turmoil of popular opinion.

Years ago, Jan and I returned to the States after a brief season of living in the West Indies. We thought our time in missions was over. We were surprised and excited when God opened a door of ministry that involved collaborating

51

and partnering with pastors who were mentors and close friends. We thought we would be putting down roots. We never dreamed that exactly two years later we would be headed for Europe on a mission's trip that would last four years.

When God opened the door to Europe, we went through a painful process of letting go. No quick and shallow response was adequate for a decision this complex. We heard a clear call to go to Europe, yet we had planned a much longer stay where we were—perhaps an indefinite stay.

The timing confused us, but revelation is not nervous about timing. It is sourced from eternity without the pressure of time.

The deeper issue had to do with our hearts of obedience. Calling and timing were important, but would we obey, or would we dismiss what we were hearing because of our love, honor, and commitment for long-term friendships and our new-found friends who had become family? The deeper issue was the most important one. Some of our friends in the church did not question our hearts, but they did question our decision. Other friends disconnected, and we understood their struggle because we also felt torn.

We had learned long before—and believed with all our hearts—that the biggest and deepest issue was obedience to God's voice. As a result, any personal obstacle or preference that arose during that period seemed to solidify the steps we were to take, rather than dissuade us. Each time, our answer was, "Yes, Lord."

Some of the pain from that decision to obey remained—in varying degrees—over many years. But the fruit of our obedience has lasted far longer.

Whenever I have made quick and visceral responses, I have found that my first answer was generally to the issues I was facing on the surface instead of the deeper God-issue He wanted to process with me. Many times I had the right answer but the wrong response. There is always something deeper when we are relating to God, and it is in the process of this relationship that He invites us to journey with Him towards the discovery of His deeper truth.

Today, give God some time to develop a deeper understanding within you about His heart for each subject that requires a response from you. In the end, the deeper God-issue you discover will always reflect His heart, not a human response.

18
EXPERIENCING THE WORD

Recently, I heard someone say how sad it was that some Christians were seeking an experience with God instead of focusing solely on Scripture. When I heard those words, something didn't feel right.

This morning, as I read through 2 Peter, I paused at the end of verse 16: "We saw his majestic splendor with our own eyes." Peter was describing his experience on the Mount of Transfiguration. He continued in verses 17-19:

> The voice from the majestic glory of God said to him, "This is my dearly loved Son, who brings me great joy." We ourselves heard that voice from heaven when we were with him on the holy mountain. Because of that experience, we have even greater confidence in the message proclaimed by the prophets.

In other words, the experience Peter had with a supernatural God on the Mount of Transfiguration released a greater confidence in the message of God.

I have taught the Word a lot over the course of my

ministry. Just doing some simple math, I figured I have taught in public church services a minimum of two times a week for thirty-plus years. That works out to be well over 3,000 messages, not including all the extra times between the weekly church services when I taught in other venues, like training seminars or conferences. The final number could easily be over 4,000 messages. That's a lot of teaching.

A friend of mine, who spent years ministering in Africa, told me about "The God-Line." In Western culture, where we place a high value on our intellect and our ability to understand and define all that takes place around us, the God-Line is just below our head. If we can't understand it with our mind, it is suspect and must remain below the line. In many African cultures, and most of the world not dominated by a Greek way of thinking, the God-Line is above the head. In these cultures, all of life is spiritual. There is no separation between teaching and experience.

When Jesus sent out The Seventy in Luke 10, He empowered them to do the experiential part of life with Jesus. In verse 9, he said to them, "Heal the sick, and tell them, 'The Kingdom of God is near you now.'" These first disciples not only shared God's Word, but they expected some kind of experience with God to follow their sharing. An experience with God is how people would see God's Word come alive.

On the Day of Pentecost, the Church was empowered to do supernatural works that would end up being processed as an experience with God. The early disciples got into trouble when they released these supernatural experiences in the cities across the Middle East. If what they believed had not become such culturally disturbing experiences, most of them would have died as old men and women without experiencing the pain of martyrdom. An experience with God that flows from the Word of God is both powerful and dangerous.

In the western world we have become really good in

our presentation of God's Word. We have become skilled presenters. I am happy for that, but I think in some cases we might have driven our religious car out onto the theological highway and simply parked it in the fast lane short of the destination called, "Experience." The Word without an experience or encounter with God is only a lecture.

When God created the heavens and the earth, the elements had an experience with God's Word and became terra firma. The formless, empty, and dark places were joined together and became something tangible, emerging as physical by-products of God's voice. When God uttered the words, "Let there be light," some powerful interaction took place—and this was just with natural elements. Imagine what happens when the Word of God is released into a human being?

Whether God's Word is preached from a pulpit or spoken prophetically on a street corner, we should have an experience when the Word enters our life.

God will expose us to experiences that we might find uncomfortable—experiences that are outside our comfort zone or tradition. Have you ever wondered why this happens? I think I have part of the answer. God allows this to take place so He can work on the gate of our heart.

The heart-gate is that place within us that can hinder or release our ability to experience more of God. Gates can swing open or shut. As the writer of Proverbs said in 4:23, "Guard your heart above all else, for it determines the course of your life."

It is so easy to shut ourselves off from experiences because we saw someone do something that put us off. We close the gate to our heart and then retreat into what we can manage with our intellect—above the God-Line. In the end, we begin to lessen our impact in the world around us because the experience of the Word is absent from the presentation of the Word.

Peter's experience on the Mount of Transfiguration

deepened his confidence in the message that Jesus—and those who came before Him—had proclaimed.

As we study God's Word, it is good to walk in the kind of faith and obedience that will release those supernatural experiences that affirm what we have studied. We will then begin to walk in a new confidence that comes from the union of His Word and the experiences that confirm his Word through the power of the Spirit.

Peter said something about "experiences" at the start of his ministry, thirty years before he wrote his two epistles. In Acts 2:22, as he was trying to explain what had just happened on the Day of Pentecost, Peter said:

> People of Israel, listen! God publicly endorsed Jesus the Nazarene by doing powerful miracles, wonders and signs through him, as you well know.

Peter was saying that Jesus, the Word incarnate, was endorsed by God through the release of supernatural experiences. He wants to do the same thing today.

19

THE LEADERSHIP PENDULUM

I remember the first time I heard a concept that I knew was a leadership principle. I was in my twenties and studying for the ministry. A wise leader said the Church is like a pendulum: it is constantly swinging back and forth to find a place of balance. Over time, I've come to realize that this pendulum never stops but continues to swing from side to side as the Church enters and departs from different seasons of life and development.

I have lived long enough to see the Church undergo change and transition. I have seen the pendulum swing widely through areas of understanding in gender roles, the ministry of the Spirit, interpretations of God's sovereignty, and a host of other issues.

The continuous motion of the pendulum is not because God is unsettled, or even that the Church is neurotic; it is because—from our viewpoint—we only see things in part, and all of us are on a constant search for balance.

This is how the Church moves forward: we advance by reconciling imbalance. Someone once told me that the very act of walking is linked to a series of movements that have us seeking balance with each new step. To walk forward, we need to let go of our last foothold and pass through a swinging gait of imbalance to gain a new balanced foothold.

The pendulum of the Church continues to swing because in any given moment we are out of balance in our current understanding about what God is doing upon the earth. I am not saying what we currently understand is wrong; it is simply not yet fully developed, no matter how mature we think we are. There is always more than we are seeing in any given moment.

Our tendency is to park our comprehension of God and His Kingdom somewhere along the timeline of certain events or revelations that we have experienced. When this happens, we begin to build our concept of ministry around that stationary observation. The outcome of this way of thinking is that we actually stop growing and learning. Narrow vision sets in, and we begin to view life and ministry with blinders on. In this stationary posture, we can begin to construct a defensive compound from which to protect our limited understanding against any perceived change coming from outside our position.

The pendulum has been swinging throughout the entire history of the Church. I think this is actually God's plan. Growing things are never static. Motion means you are alive.

Just when I think I fully understand a point of theology, or how the Church should be led, or what the best model is for doing church on Sunday morning, God will lovingly take me to a wider and more expanded view of what He is accomplishing in His people. He does this by showing me the smallness of what I have chosen to see. Realizing the smallness of my own vision allows me to repent and begin to live in greater humility and see the value of differing opinions than the one I hold.

Realizing we don't know all things keeps us open to

expanding our circle of fellowship to include others who may not process life like us. A willingness to admit my limited understanding deconstructs the pride that comes when I think I fully see and understand all that is happening along the swinging arc of the pendulum.

I have learned a few things by watching the pendulum of understanding within the Church.

I have learned that I need to be careful to not capture and define what I think God is doing, mid-swing in the pendulum arc, and build a definition around that limited understanding. The leaders I observe, who lead from a place of peace, are not trying to get the pendulum to stop so they can define something. These leaders step back and watch the pendulum from a distance, trying to anticipate the direction God is taking His Church, and then they begin to move their lives and ministries in that direction.

I have learned that it is wise to resist the urge to park our understanding anywhere along the arc of a developing principle. Wherever we park, we become irrelevant in our ability to engage developing realities and emerging generations of leadership. To finish well means that we must remain mobile in the way we think so that past structures, preferences, ideas, etc. don't define or hinder us.

I have learned that the older a person gets the more the desire surfaces to return to "the good old days." This desire must be seen as a warning that we are not engaging the moment. We all have preferences and life-experiences that warm our hearts. Those things were never intended to lead; rather, they are to be stones of remembrance left behind along the trail of our developing journey. The destination is always ahead.

Finally, I have learned that the pendulum is a teacher. Too many times I have felt I had some current issue all figured out when God had me sit in front of the swinging pendulum and simply watch. As I watched, I realized that some of what I thought ten years ago I no longer processed the same way today. Those people and ministries I disapproved of years ago are now closer in thought and fellowship to me than ever before. The swinging pendulum has taught me to let go of snap judgments, and it has freed me to wait a while until the pendulum swings back my way with a new and clearer understanding of what is taking place in the Church.

20
A RETURN TO AWE AND AMAZEMENT

Recently, in a time of corporate prayer, I sensed the Holy Spirit ask me a question: "Are you awed by God or impressed by man?" Though this question was asked within the quiet confines of my heart, I knew it was for all who were present that day. A few minutes later, I asked the question out loud for all to hear.

I think the question surfaced, in part, because for the last few years the second chapter of Acts has opened up for me in new ways. I am seeing things in the text that I had missed on many past readings.

What I began to notice in Acts 2 was the repeated experience of people being amazed by God or awed by His presence. Whenever the Word repeats something I take special notice.

The entire city of Jerusalem was affected by the supernatural uproar caused on the Day of Pentecost. Acts 2:6 reads:

When they heard the loud noise, everyone came

running, and they were bewildered to hear their own languages being spoken by the believers.

Verse 7 goes on to say that those who came running "were completely amazed." This was not a partial amazement, but a total and complete amazement at what God was doing. Today, we might say, "They were blown away!"

After declaring how awesome it was to hear the wonderful things God had done in their native tongue, the text continues in verse 12: "They stood there amazed and perplexed. 'What can this mean?' they asked each other." They were stopped in their tracks by the experience—they just stood there—amazed.

Peter went on to preach his famous Day of Pentecost message. After the message, the amazed listeners asked in verse 37, "Brothers, what should we do?" Peter told them to repent of their sins, turn to God and get baptized, and then they would receive the amazing Spirit of God. After Peter finished speaking, 3,000 awestruck people joined the Church.

This amazing work of God did not stop on the Day of Pentecost. God's work birthed a community of faith who were ruined for anything that wasn't awe-inspiring. A normal and predictable Christianity would not hold the attention of this group.

Later in Acts 2, the believers formed a community and devoted themselves to the apostles' teaching, fellowship, common meals, and prayer. Verse 43 says, "A deep sense of awe came over them all, and the apostles performed many miraculous signs and wonders." Pentecost was not a terminal event locked in history. The event of Pentecost began unfolding forward into the developing history of the Church, and it has continued for more than 2,000 years.

I used to think the signs and wonders produced the awe within this first community of faith (vs. 43), but the text says the miracles followed the awe that had come over them. The awe of God first fell in their midst much like the Spirit had fallen just days before on the Day of Pentecost. Once the awe arrived, the miracles soon followed. This awe of God falls into our midst because it comes from Heaven, not from what we do on earth. God's works are awe-inspiring and leave people standing in amazement—that is truly amazing and awe-inspiring.

21
SPIRITUAL ENVIRONMENTALISTS

The word "environmentalist" can make you happy or angry depending on how you view politics and culture. Actually, it is a very good word when used in conjunction with God and His Kingdom. Environmentalists are concerned with the long-term health of the place where they live. The same is true for a spiritual environmentalist within the Church.

People have asked me how to create an environment where the Spirit of God is free to dwell among us. This question was not asked regarding the personal possession of the Spirit that all believers enjoy. This question refers to that corporate experience with Jesus that takes places when two or more gather in His name, whether in a scheduled church meeting or over coffee at Starbucks.

In Matthew 18:20 Jesus said, "For where two or three gather together as my followers, I am there among them." This revelation of God's presence, where more than one person is present, is what we mean when we say, "the manifest presence of God." We carry Him within each of us all the time, but when we come together, His presence is "manifest" among us in a different way: in the midst of us. This "in the midst" place is where we are supposed to work as spiritual environmentalists to clean up the junk and sludge of our own brokenness that is not only polluting our lives but the lives of others as well.

When I talk with leaders within the Church, I tell them that they are responsible to create an environment where the Holy Spirit is free to make Jesus known. This environment becomes a reality when the priority of the local church is not growth, miracles, or even salvations. All three of these are wonderful by-products of a healthy environment and are very important, but they are not our first priority. Our first priority as the Church is to host God's presence. Anything that hinders this hosting of His presence will hinder the work God wants to do in our midst. Heaven's environment is one of love, the fruit of the Spirit, relationship, communion, oneness, and honor.

This healthy environment becomes a reality when we personally choose to remove the toxins of self and striving and give God back a garden of life where He is free to walk and minister among us. This environment becomes a reality when we follow polluted streams of personal runoff to their source and deal with our wrong heart attitudes that will eventually breed death, not life.

The Second Adam—Jesus—did not redeem us back to the events and curses that immediately followed the sin of Eden. Our Second Adam redeemed us back to the realities of Eden, before the Fall, where He could walk with us unhindered through a beautiful and unpolluted place. This is the ministry of a Spiritual Environmentalist.

22

BE CAREFUL WITH FIRST READS

Recently, I read a blog article written by a very respected young leader. He is well read and well educated. He does things with excellence. He has become noticed for all of these attributes and rightfully so.

Because we are all in a hurry from time to time, I did a quick read through his blog. I missed what he was saying and began to carry an offense based on my quick, narrow, and judgmental investment in his article. I found myself wanting to correct him in a public forum.

For an entire day I carried a low-grade offense. I was thinking about how to correct this young man. Maybe I would Tweet a reference to what he wrote or post something on Facebook. This went on all day until, later that evening, the Lord had me reread the article. I could hardly believe it: on the second read, I realized that I was terribly wrong and misinformed. This young author was saying something that was not only accurate but much appreciated by me for its content. My hurried read was blind. I am so thankful I did not respond out of my narrow field of vision.

I came away from this embarrassing revelation learning a few things about myself. I also came away with some things we all need to be reminded of from time to time:

A First Read is Just That: A First Read

Rarely do we ever grasp a person's true intent the first time around. We owe it to each other, and to the Church at large, to "read" things again to make sure we are actually correct in our observations. And even then, we should not forget that we only see things partially.

We All Carry Reactive Baggage

This young author was touching on something dear to my heart. I was defensive about this truth and had anointed myself its protector. Our reactive baggage is usually packed with items from our broken history and unresolved personal issues. Reactive baggage cannot be trusted to speak the truth; it needs to be laundered.

Believe the Best

When we read what people have written or when we hear about what they have spoken or done, we owe them the honor of believing the best about them and not making snap judgments. Our judgments put people in a place where we don't have to engage them. This results in separation. God is not happy with separation because it breaks fellowship.

My response revealed that God has more work to do inside my heart. We never arrive at a place where we can't be corrected. I had to tell the Lord how sorry I was regarding my response and admit to Him that I needed His help.

WAIT BEFORE YOU POUNCE

It only takes a little more investment of time to do something right. A wrong response, and the resulting hurt, may never be retrievable if you let ill-informed judgments lead your response to what you do not understand.

AFFIRM WHAT HAS BEEN WRITTEN OR SAID

You don't have to tell the person all the facts about your personal struggle. A simple affirmation about what he or she has written, said, or done accomplishes two things. First, if just feels good. And second, it can open up a relational bridge with this person that would never have existed had you not corrected your wrong attitude.

Years ago, Jerry Cook wrote a book titled, *A Few Things I've Learned Since I Knew It All*. His book title described his attitude adjustment. I don't like the feeling that comes when I think I know it all and find out I didn't know as much as I thought. A good "God-correction" is like taking a spiritual bath. You come out clean all over. In the end it, it feels good.

23

A 'BASS-ACKWARDS' APPROACH TO MINISTRY

On my summer breaks as a young boy, I used to help out in my dad's construction business. Dad built houses, and he also owned a house moving company. I was always working each summer.

Dad would assign a project to me and then go elsewhere on the job site. When he returned, he would often say, "Son, you got that one 'bass-ackwards.'" That famous line meant I was doing something opposite to how it should be done. He would show me my mistake and then share the remedy to the problem. He wouldn't do the work; he simply showed me how to undo the "bass-ackwards" nature of my first attempt.

If dad were here today, he would look at how some of us pastors do ministry and he would say we are turned around. He would say to return to Ephesians and read chapter four again and recognize that our job is to "equip God's people to do his work and build up the church" (vs. 12), not to do the ministry ourselves.

In fact, dad would go on to say that the growth of the Church is never the pastor's responsibility. God grows things that really last, we don't. The people we have equipped and built up are the ones who will share their faith and help lead others into a living relationship with God. They will be the ones who invite people to our community of faith to experience spiritual growth and maturity.

I think dad's view about the "bass-ackwardness" of a young boy's construction job applies to church leadership. We should do our best to train, equip, and build up God's people, and then rest and wait for the fruit to come. The seeds of our investment in people need time to germinate. It is in the restless waiting that we can become impatient and begin to reverse God's order of discipleship.

When we make the decision to properly reorder how we see the Church, our levels of stress and performance will diminish greatly. The things of life and calling will naturally reposition themselves in a healthy God-order that won't be so "bass-ackwards."

24
RISKING THE MESSAGE

When I finished my weekly prayer hike one summer day, I stopped at our town's outdoor concert area, The Britt. The Britt is a performance venue positioned on a sloping, grass hillside. Each summer, some of the best musicians on earth come to play there.

The month of August is devoted to classical concerts. Most mornings in August, the orchestra practices for the coming evening concert. Sitting in the shade of a pine tree on The Britt hillside is a great way to cool down after a long hike.

That summer day, I sat beneath a tree and heard the Lord say to me, "If your voice is not perceived as crying from a wilderness place, you are probably not announcing the coming of the Lord." The reference to the ministry of John the Baptist was obvious to me, but there was more. As I meditated on what I thought the Lord said, I began to realize that when God is about to do a new thing, He will give someone a word that may seem as strange and unusual as the words associated with the ministry of John the Baptist.

New and unusual instructions from the Lord can be dismissed because they don't resemble the sound of what we are currently hearing. Commonness can dull our hearing over time because we have a tendency to tune out all but the familiar.

Each of us wants to appear "normal," but we must release that need if we are going to allow God to speak to us and through us the new things He wants to do. We spend a lot of time crafting our self-image. This crafting can radically change what God initially intended for our lives. Self-crafting a personal image typically hides the real person. Jerry Cook recently told a group of us that the problem with our self-image is that it is usually a fake.

A lot of the Bible says the saints of God simply told it like it was and let the words fall where they may. For some this can become a license to be rude and abusive. That's not what John the Baptist was—he was simply honest, truthful and obedient.

Many times I try to figure out the varied perceptions people may have about me. We all do this. God wants us to end that fear-based way of living and risk the loss of acceptance where our words may cause an interruption in a slumbering culture.

John the Baptist shouted his message from the wilderness. The entire population of Jerusalem, estimated to be in the hundreds of thousands, left the city in response to his voice and walked out into the wilderness to listen. When they got to the wilderness, the messenger looked as strange as the message he shouted, yet what happened was profoundly supernatural. Heaven opened up, a dove came down, and the voice of God spoke. I will risk my image and my cultural status if these are the results obedience brings when we speak as one shouting from the wilderness.

25
CRITICS AND CRISIS

It seems in each season of breakthrough two things show up: critics and crisis. At our best, we will never be able to please all people all the time. I know that it was a rude awakening the first time I realized that not all people agreed with me.

Critics, for the most part, do their critique behind closed doors. This kind of criticism is fueled in private without you being present. This criticism will grow and remain unchallenged until it is discovered. Once discovered, it must be challenged in love. Unless dealt with, it will spread like a cancer without the "medicine" of truth to confront it. Small groups of "friends" can gather around this kind of criticism and require of each other an alignment with their toxic point of view. An emerging crisis of relationship begins to develop because it is being fueled by this cancerous criticism. This kind of battle needs to be fought based on rules of engagement from the Kingdom of God, not the kingdom of this world.

In the book of Judges there is a re-occurring theme. Israel walks in sin, and God sends judges to expose their sin and call them to repentance. After these confrontations with their national sin, Israel would repent and begin to live in peace. Before long Israel would return to their sin, and the process would start all over again.

A man named Jephthah emerged as a judge over Israel. In one instance, he was dealing with the king of the Ammonites over a land dispute. When Jephthah delivered the word of the Lord to this king, the king paid no attention to what was said. As a result, Israel went to battle with the Ammonites and destroyed them.

Jephthah spoke to the Ammonite king before the battle and said, "Let the Lord, who is judge, decide today which of us is right—Israel or Ammon" (Judges 11:27).

The word Jephthah delivered to the Ammonite king would not be confirmed in its delivery; it would be confirmed in battle. Words of the Lord are confirmed in battle. Where and how we choose to do battle has a huge effect on the outcome and confirmation of God's word in our lives.

God is the only one who can righteously decide and define true victory. Even in a time of criticism, those being criticized have something to learn from their critics. If you find yourself in the midst of a season of critics and crisis it is time to look again at the battle armor of a New Covenant believer and to make sure those protective coverings are in place.

We are called to stand fully armored and to let God fight for us. This battle is fought from a stationary posture. Paul described this battle armor in Ephesians 6 as the belt of truth, the breastplate of righteousness, the shoes of peace, the shield of faith, the helmet of salvation and the sword of God's Word.

Taking a stationary posture in battle does not mean that we don't speak the truth in love and confront sin. We speak from a place of truth, righteousness, peace, faith, salvation, and God's Word. We don't let the battle draw us into the battle. In this kind of warfare, we evaluate our words and our response to our critics through the filter of our Spirit-empowered armament.

The weapons of our warfare are not drawn from the armory of this earth. These weapons are imported across the border between heaven and earth. These weapons look powerless to the natural mind, but they are what God will use to bring down the spirit of criticism and turn the crisis into victory.

Critics can bring to their acts of war-like criticism unresolved sin, brokenness, and limited observations. These unresolved personal issues create a lens through which they view you. We all do this. Sometimes these critics can bring an element of truth hidden within their criticism.

What you and I can do is to step into a supernatural level of trust that hands the outcome of our crisis—and the critics themselves—over to God. None of this is personal even though it feels deeply personal. God loves your critics as much as He loves you. God's victory will always look different than what we have planned because our plan can have personal vindication in the mix. God's plan is different; it brings Him glory.

When we allow God to decide what is right, a sense of rest comes because we are not expending our thoughts and energy on the preservation of our self-image. This kind of rest is deep inside our soul where the criticism and crisis cannot do battle once we close the door to its entry. This kind of rest is a spiritual resistance that confounds the real enemy (the enemy is not people) and puts him to flight.

I prayed the following prayer during a season of personal criticism and crisis. It helped me reset my heart and maybe it will help you.

"Lord, this criticism hurts. My wounds feel overwhelming. I don't understand why this is taking place. I want to run to the battle and scorch my critics with words of self-vindication. Forgive me. I ask you to first examine me before I examine others. See if there is any hurtful way in me. In this crisis, I want you to do another battle within me in those private places of my own pride and fear that this crisis has brought to light. I choose to rest in the knowledge that you will decide who is 'right.'"

26

GOD'S ALARM CLOCK

My weekends are important times for me. These are the times that our church gathers and when I teach. I take them seriously. I always want to be fresh for Sunday morning so I can give my best to God and His people. As the weekend rolls around, I try to unclutter my schedule so that Saturday night I get to bed early to be well rested for Sunday morning.

On one particular Saturday morning, I became wide-awake at 3:30 a.m. I thought this was not good. I tried to go back to sleep, but I couldn't. I didn't want to awaken Jan with my rustling in bed, so I quietly got up.

Instead of making the noise required to start the coffee maker, I decided to get in our car and head out to a donut shop I knew that opened at 4:00 a.m. I don't normally eat donuts, but on this particular morning my palate called for one.

Arriving at the donut shop, I went through the drive-through and ordered an apple fritter and a large coffee. I drove around to the parking lot of the donut shop, turned on the radio, and had my breakfast as I sat in the darkness. When I finished the coffee and fritter I actually felt pretty good—not tired or groggy. Then I drove home.

The next day, Sunday, I wasn't tired at church, even though my normal routine had been disturbed. I had a great workweek, and life went on as normal.

The next Saturday morning, the same thing happened. I became wide-awake, again—way too early to just lay in bed. I knew what to do this time and headed for the donut shop. When I was done, I thought I would drive to the church since it was close by.

When I arrived at the church is was about 4:30 a.m. I entered the back door that leads into the sanctuary and immediately sensed that hush you experience in a forest when all man-made noise is absent. I stood there and began to soak in the abiding presence of God that accompanies a structure that week after week is dedicated to God, a place where sounds of worship and praise have filled the air for years. It was like I was being bathed in warm oil. I prayed and asked God to bless the coming Sunday service, and then I drove home.

The next Saturday I was awakened again. This time I began to realize God was waking me from my sleep. No alarm clock, just the Lord wanting time with one of his sons. As I write, this Saturday morning routine has been going on for the last thirteen years. I set no alarm, and He faithfully awakens me each week. I now spend close to three hours with God each Saturday morning. I look forward to this time; I minister to Him and He ministers to me as the city sleeps.

One of the things I do each Saturday is to stand before the empty sanctuary and talk out loud with God about the Sunday message I will preach the next day. I go over my sermon notes and let God make any adjustments He desires. I also bring my breakfast, and we eat together.

On Saturday mornings, I walk through the sanctuary

and lay hands on each chair and pray for those who will attend our worship services the next day. I declare hope and destiny over the church. I confront dark spirits. I do the work of a priest of God.

For all the years I have done this, I have told my staff that the church facility is off-limits for those several hours. They have scheduled church life around my weekly time with God. The church knows about this special time and honors it.

This protected and reserved time has allowed me to function in complete freedom with God. There was a time God had me jog throughout our facility shouting prayers. Another time I lay prostrate on the platform and moaned His heart for His people. Once, a twenty-foot ladder was left in the sanctuary by the facilities team who were in the process of adjusting the platform lighting. God asked me to climb all the way to the top of the ladder and prophetically declare His heart over His people. Being alone with God has allowed me a new level of freedom and intimacy.

What I have come to realize is that God wants time alone with us. He is so passionate about this time that He will awaken us from our regular patterns of life and carve out time normally given to sleep and work and say, "Come and be with me." If we will walk with Him into these times, we will enter those places where we will experience the quiet hush of His presence. Those times will become the highlights of our week.

27
LIVING ON BOTH SIDES OF "AND"

Whenever the word "and" is used in the Scriptures, I pay attention. When God uses this word, He is trying to connect things for our benefit.

When Jesus walked the earth, He was modeling for the Church what we would become after His death, resurrection, and ascension.

A caution should exist in our lives when we read the word "and" in God's Word and then choose to live on either side of that word and feel OK with it. The word "and" is a connecting word that says both sides are to be embraced.

It is interesting to look at a few occurrences of "and" in the New Testament. In Matthew 4, the word "and" describes the ministry of Jesus. Notice my added italics:

> Jesus traveled throughout the region of Galilee, teaching in the synagogues *and* announcing the Good News about the Kingdom. *And* he healed every kind of disease *and* illness. News about him spread as far as Syria, *and* people soon began bringing to him all who were sick. *And* whatever their sickness or disease, or if they were

demon possessed or epileptic or paralyzed—he healed them all. Large crowds followed him wherever he went—people from Galilee, the Ten Towns, Jerusalem, from all over Judea, *and* from east of the Jordan River" (vs 23-25).

I'd like to draw attention to one "and" in particular here. Notice that Jesus announced and taught the Good News about the Kingdom of God, *and* He healed every kind of disease and illness. The full expression of the ministry of Jesus was not an either-or situation. He was not either an evangelical or Pentecostal expression of the Church—He was both.

In another text where "and" is used, John the Baptist was waiting in prison about to be served up as a macabre dinner gesture. This was the same man who was there at the Baptism of Jesus when the heavens opened up, the dove of God's presence descended, and the very voice of God spoke to those present. It doesn't get more vivid than what took place that day. But John was now having some doubts about Jesus. Prisons, both in the natural and the spirit realm, can challenge our perception of reality.

John sent His disciples to ask Jesus the question, "Are you the Messiah we've been expecting, or should we keep looking for someone else?" (Matthew 11:3). Jesus sent a response back to John's prison cell that allowed John to die in peace knowing that Jesus was truly the Messiah:

> Jesus told them, "Go back to John and tell him what you have heard and seen—the blind see, the lame walk, the lepers are cured, the deaf hear, the dead are raised to life, *and* the Good News is being preached to the poor. And tell him, 'God blesses those who do not turn away because of me'" (vs. 4-5, italics mine).

What does this mean? A balanced ministry will live on both sides of "and." Some people are more comfortable simply preaching the salvation message. Jesus wasn't.

Others feel like they should only press into signs and wonders. Jesus didn't. He did both, and so should we. The expansion of God's Kingdom, through signs and wonders, has to walk hand in hand with populating heaven with new believers. If we assign either side of "and" to a less than visible position, then we will not be walking in the fullness of His assignment for us as the Church.

Life is a constantly swinging pendulum that moves from one imbalance to another. Our pendulum moves over God's perfect will with each pass. The shorter the cycle of that pendulum swing, the more mature a believer becomes. If the pendulum gets hung up on either side of "and," the Church can look like a one-legged man trying to win a race by hopping down the race track instead of the well-trained and balanced athlete sprinting forward on two strong and conditioned legs.

28
I DON'T BELIEVE IN THAT

I have a friend who writes some profound things on his online daily devotional. A few months ago, he wrote that he was not going to use the word "awesome" anymore, except to describe God. My friend's commitment on personal vocabulary is a wise word in a world where we say, "I love baseball," and in the same breath, "I love God." In our haphazard use of words, we sometimes dilute their true meanings.

A few months ago, I had a conversation with someone who had been in a meeting where the leader of the service was moving in a free and bold approach to God. Physical healings were taking place and people were being set free. Some people had very visible reactions to the power of God. The person who was telling me about this meeting felt uncomfortable. He said he was not sure he believed in what he was seeing.

When God moves in unusual ways sometimes people will say, "I don't believe in that!" They might be focusing on the style of what is taking place and not the substance of what God is actually doing. We all do this from time to time. When something different is happening around us, maybe something that makes us uncomfortable, we want to find a place to position that experience and define it so we can deal with it. Sometimes we say, "I don't believe in that!" but what we are really saying is: "I'm uncomfortable."

Today, I have been processing how to respond better to people when they make such comments. The next time someone says to me, "I don't believe in that!" I would like to be more nurturing in my response. Maybe I could respond with words like these: "You just said that you don't believe in what you just saw. Maybe we should reserve the word 'belief' for things that deal with the person of God, His Son, the Holy Spirit, and the way of salvation. Maybe our use of the word 'believe' is getting confused with what we like, don't like, or feel uncomfortable with."

As I reread some of the Early Church creeds recently, I noticed that the authors were wise enough to keep the creeds simple and focused on God and His Church instead of linking belief to personal preferences that can be jaded by our fears and uncomfortable experiences. That seems like a good practice to me.

29
RESTORED FLIGHT

One afternoon I was driving home from my office to pack for a conference that my wife and I planned to attend in California the next day. On the commute home, my route takes me through some beautiful farmland and rolling hills.

On one long section of road, I noticed the brake lights of cars beginning to light up ahead of me, so I slowed down. After a few moments, I saw what was causing the traffic to slow. A bird had been struck by a passing car and was wounded and flapping its wings in the middle of the road. It was trying to fly again. Helplessness in any wounded creature is sad. This bird God had created to fly had apparently broken its back on impact with a passing car and could not flap its wings hard enough to get airborne again. Birds don't do well against cars. Birds don't belong on highway surfaces; they belong in the air.

We can all end up in places we don't belong. In the springtime, when kings went to war, David stayed home and fell into sin. Despite all the mess of David's life, God still called him a man after His own heart.

After his denial of Christ, Peter went back to fishing for fish instead of fishing for men. Jesus had to restore him so he could fish for men once again. Peter's record-breaking swim from the boat to shore reveals how much he wanted to be with Jesus.

When we really blow it, we think everything is over. The greatest failures in our lives can actually become the very places from which our true destiny emerges. A life without the hope of restoration destroys people. A life with hope makes us write Psalms of joy and preach powerful sermons on the Day of Pentecost.

As Jan and I arrived at the conference and completed our registration, we were assigned a day and a time to receive personal prophecy. Each registered attendee was given an appointment that would take place at some point in the next three days. These "prophecy booths" are rich times of sitting with loving people who prophesy the heart of God. At this particular conference of 800, the process of getting all these people into fifteen-minute time slots was something to behold. Our appointment was for the next morning.

As we waited in line, the group scheduled to go before us was getting ready to enter their appointment. Then I heard a voice I knew. I turned my head and confirmed that the voice belonged to a prominent leader of a world-impacting church. He and his wife were just six feet away from us.

This was a leader of a large church organization who had stepped into sin and whose name had been plastered all over the news.

When I looked over at this leader, I felt the compassion of God well up in me. One of my first thoughts was: what guts, strength, and humility were at work for this man and his wife to get in line with the rest of us who also needed a word of hope from God. All of a sudden, I loved God more. I loved the leader more. I loved the Church more. I loved the ministry who hosted this conference more for having such a culture of honor. I was able to love more because hope was in the house.

As I stood in line waiting, I remembered the bird in the roadway from the day before—a creature that had been wounded and was trying to fly again. That bird never left its nest as a chick with plans to someday fly into the grill of a fast-moving car.

Birds don't belong on roadways. Pastors don't belong in sinful situations, but sad things do happen. The surprise is not that we do sinful things. The surprise is that there could be a place where broken lives can fly again. Part of me is sad that the latter is a surprise.

The wounded bird in the roadway probably died later that day. But that morning, waiting in line for a personal word of hope, I felt that this man would one day fly again.

30

THE BOTTOM LINE OF EVERYTHING

I like getting to the bottom line of things. If I know the bottom line in a given situation, I know where I stand—and I know what I am required to do even when life is confusing and seems directionless.

In Mark 12:28, a man came to Jesus with a legitimate question. He asked, "Of all the commandments, which is the most important?" In other words: what is the bottom line? Here's the context:

> One of the teachers of religious law was standing there listening to the debate. He realized that Jesus had answered well, so he asked, "Of all the commandments, which is the most important?" Jesus replied, "The most important commandment is this: 'Listen, O Israel! The Lord our God is the one and only Lord. And you must love the Lord your God with all your heart, all your soul, all your mind, and all your strength.' The second is equally important: 'Love your neighbor as yourself.' No other commandment is greater than these." The teacher of religious law replied, "Well said, Teacher. You have spoken the truth by saying that there is only one God and no other. And I know it is important to love him

with all my heart and all my understanding and all my strength, and to love my neighbor as myself. This is more important than to offer all of the burnt offerings and sacrifices required in the law." Realizing how much the man understood, Jesus said to him, "You are not far from the Kingdom of God." And after that, no one dared to ask him any more questions.

The man asking the question actually got it right. Jesus realized this man understood truth and told him he wasn't far from the Kingdom.

When the western Church shares its reason for existence, we use phrases like, "Loving God and Loving People" to define our calling. In fact I have used those words myself. But there is more. The Great Commandment really has three parts. Jesus stated another component that we often overlook in the definition of the Great Commandment.

Before we can love God and love people, we need to understand what Jesus said just before, and in conjunction with, the statements about loving God and people. Jesus said, "'Listen, O Israel! The Lord our God is the one and only Lord." Some translators have rendered this to read, "The one and only absolute God." Jesus was quoting from Deuteronomy 6 a phrase devout Jews still quote today.

If you follow the logic of what Jesus quoted, He was essentially saying, "Listen, people, this one and only absolute God has a one and only Son, and my name is Jesus, and I am standing right in front of you."

Some in the Church love God and love people without publicly mentioning the name of the one and only Son of the one and only Lord. It is too easy to simply blend in with the good deeds of an NGO or a local service club and lose the distinctive personality that drives our efforts.

For 2,000 years of Church history, people have been martyred because of the name of Jesus. While the Church has been called to do good works—to feed the poor, to build houses, and to serve the hungry in soup lines—no one was ever killed because they handed out a sandwich to someone. People were martyred because of the name of the Son of the one and only true God who confronted the darkness of a culture.

The good works are important—please do them, but the work and the message of the Church is about the Name. The Name redeems, not the works of the redeemed. All that we do has to be connected to the Name.

When I came to Medford, Oregon to pastor our church, I noticed that we had a stack of cards on the lobby counter. On the cards were the printed words of St. Francis of Assisi: "Preach the Gospel at all times, and when necessary use words." I am sure that when those words were penned they were powerful and relevant. They still are in many ways. But I had a problem with them in the context of our current, American church culture.

One night, when I was alone in the lobby, I threw those cards in the trash. I threw them away because for the previous four years, I had been working in Eastern Europe, where I saw a Church that had survived horrible persecution because of the Name. To even whisper the Name in the public square could mean prison and in some cases death.

Jesus said in Mark 9:41: "If anyone gives you even a cup of water because you belong to the Messiah, I tell you the truth, that person will surely be rewarded." The giving of just a cup of water contained a reward when it was attached to the name of Jesus.

The Great Commandment is about selling out to God in totality and doing the good works in the name of Jesus. Without attaching the name of Jesus to the cup of water, we blend in and become just another nice voice in the crowd.

It was the Name that got the Apostles martyred. It is the Name that still makes the demons of hell shudder today. It is the Name that changes the atmosphere of a cocktail party. It is the Name that has the power to do the impossible.

The Church has been called into the market place to be a witness to the one and only true God and to live fully committed lives in the power and influence of His Son, Jesus. Our calling card in culture must have His name printed on the front of the card, or else we are not fully living out the Greatest Commandment.

31

WE NEVER REALLY GET PAST JERUSALEM

As Jesus was about to leave the earth after His resurrection, He set in motion the final preparation for His disciples to carry out His mission. Pentecost was coming soon. In Acts 1:8, Jesus said to His disciples:

> "But you will receive power when the Holy Spirit comes upon you. And you will be my witnesses, telling people about me everywhere—in Jerusalem, throughout Judea, in Samaria, and to the ends of the earth."

I used to look at these words only as the progressive unfolding of the Church geographically. In one sense, that is true. What started in Jerusalem migrated from region to region, and now the earth has been covered with the witness of Jesus Christ. But there was more to that understanding that I was about to learn.

When we lived in Berlin, Germany I was preparing a teaching on missions for a group of pastors in an Eastern European nation. As I prepared to speak, the Spirit spoke to me: "You never leave Jerusalem." I found that statement odd, since I knew what was in the text. The Spirit was about to deepen my understanding of the mission of the Church.

When we send out missionaries to the ends of the earth or to an inner-city mission, we are sending people to those places to raise up leaders and plant churches that will eventually reach their city. For those being reached, their city is their personal Jerusalem. For the last 2,000 years, these "Jerusalem" cities have been found in places described as the "ends of the earth." In that sense, we are sending people to distant lands or people groups to train them to reach their own Jerusalem.

I spent some years overseas in different nations, and I can remember the first few times I traveled outside the U.S.A. It was exciting. It was really an "uttermost part of the earth" kind of experience. As those experiences became more frequent, and eventually became a ministry assignment overseas, I realized that the people of Berlin, Germany lived in their own Jerusalem. Berlin was not a distant land to them. It was distant to me. Berlin was home to the Berliners. The people of Kingston, Jamaica lived in their own Jerusalem. To the residents of Kingston, Kingston was their Jerusalem, not a Judea or a distant Samaria.

If I was going to be faithful to my calling, I would have to go to a distant land and actually see it through the eyes of those living in their Jerusalem. I was not going to those places to help them reach an unfamiliar place. They lived, worked, and ministered in a familiar Jerusalem. Jerusalem is all around us. It is the street we live on. It is the workplace we enter each day. It is the parking lot we walk across to attend a worship service.

An indicator that we have grown in our calling and Kingdom assignment is when we begin to see the need to invest and serve beyond the boundaries of our own Jerusalem. A spiritually healthy individual or ministry is always looking beyond its own sphere of influence towards

Judea, Samaria, and to the ends of the earth. As we faithfully serve the assignment God has given to each of us, He will begin to stir up that Acts 1:8 Spirit-breathed calling to go as His witnesses to help people repeat the same process in their city. In one sense, we never really get past a Jerusalem mindset as we journey towards the ends of the earth. Wherever we go, we will eventually arrive in someone's Jerusalem.

32

WORD, WORSHIP, AND THE WITNESS OF THE SPIRIT

Roy Hicks Jr., who is now with the Lord, said something to a group of us pastors-in-training about thirty years ago that I will never forget. Someone asked what Roy used to determine if a church meeting was successful. Roy fired off the words, "Word, worship, and the witness of the Spirit." Those words became the desired benchmark for the last thirty years of my ministry. When those three ingredients were in place, our meetings always carried the weight of heaven.

Without a doubt, the Word is the written Word of God. All that we do must be strained through the *logos* Word of God to make sure we are in line with truth. There is another word, and that is the *rhema* word of God. These are the words spoken by the Word of God Himself that may come in forms other than a leather-bound bible. These *rhema* words work hand in hand with God's written Word. They enhance each other. To have a gathering of the Church and not have God speaking to us is foreign not only to the history of the Church, but also to the very nature of God. He loves to speak to His kids.

Worship is our highest calling. Our lives, our words, our ministries—everything is to be an act of worship. In a contemporary church service, worship often looks like a worship team, music, and singing. When Roy mentioned worship, he never intended us to understand this to mean something we don't participate in. Worship should draw us out and make us feel vulnerable. Worship is never to be a performance I watch from my chair. Worship can only be done by people who know the One they are worshipping. If our worship is not allowing the release of God's Spirit to bring His gifts and fruit into our midst, then we are missing one of the greatest joys in life.

The witness of God's Spirit is the one where it's easy to let things slide. The gathering of the Church is just that: the Church assembled. I never did understand the contemporary definition of a church gathering that primarily focused on non-believers' needs. That was something I always thought the Church did in the streets. The Church gathering was the place where we came to get healed up and equipped to go out into our communities and see the work of God in power and demonstration.

The witness of God's presence in His Church is seen in innumerable ways. We want to be sensitive to the voice of the Lord and take time to listen to Him and make room for any adjustment or direction. We listen for direction before and during a gathering. I often minister right after worship or even in the middle of a sermon when I take time to pray over the people or have them pray over each other. I may be directed to prophesy the Word of the Lord or have someone else prophesy.

The gathering of believers is a time when the Church needs to experience the witness of God's Spirit so that when they do venture out into the streets they can actually live like the people who are recorded in the Book of Acts: those who carried a personal experience—a witness of the Spirit—out into the city.

The Word, Worship, and the Witness of God's Spirit will redefine what we do when we gather, and together they will give us the goods we need to minister once we leave the church building.

33

THE MIRACULOUS ENVIRONMENT OF HONOR

In political seasons, I sometimes cringe when people speak. Some very foolish and dishonoring words can be spoken in the heat of political rhetoric. An election cycle is a unique opportunity for the Church to create a healing environment by extending honor—in word and deed—to all people.

To honor means to value someone or something. Value conveys honor. Honor is only possible when we see the value that God has placed on people. He came to die for all people. The value of a person causes us to honor them for who they are in God's redemptive plan. Honor is not something we give based on a person's performance or something we give only to those who deserve or earn it. Honor flows from timeless eternity before any of us can perform rightly. Honor is an act of grace.

Who should we honor?

Romans 12:10: "Take delight in honoring each other." Some think this only applies between believers. If that were the case, then most of our modern missions enterprise would have shut down. Missionaries are being sent each day on missions of mercy to honor those who don't know God's love—those who feel abandoned and alone. The very act of taking the Gospel to people groups is a journey of honor. People see the heart of God most clearly when someone steps out from the noise of the condemning crowd and says something that honors them as a unique creation of God.

Jesus visited His hometown twice. Both times the people rejected Him. The Word tells us that because the people were without honor, He could not perform many miracles among them.

Mark 6 records one of these visits by Jesus to Nazareth:

> Jesus left that part of the country and returned with his disciples to Nazareth, his hometown. The next Sabbath he began teaching in the synagogue, and many who heard him were amazed. They asked, "Where did he get all this wisdom and the power to perform such miracles?" Then they scoffed, "He's just a carpenter, the son of Mary and the brother of James, Joseph, Judas, and Simon. And his sisters live right here among us." They were deeply offended and refused to believe in him (vs. 1-3).

The word for "offended" in verse 3 means "to be caught in a trap." The people of Nazareth were caught in their own trap of judgment constructed from their personal opinions about Jesus. Some said that He was just a carpenter; they judged His vocation. Others said He was just the son of Mary; they judged His family. Still others said His sisters lived right there with them; they judged Jesus based on their familiarity with Him.

Most of the time, we only see people on the surface, though their occupation, family background, political affiliation, or personal brokenness. God sees people differently. God sees people with the finished product in view. The bridge between brokenness and the finished product is constructed with words and actions of honor.

Then Jesus told them, "A prophet is honored everywhere except in his own hometown and among his relatives and his own family." And because of their unbelief, he couldn't do any miracles among them except to place his hands on a few sick people and heal them. And he was amazed at their unbelief. Then Jesus went from village to village, teaching the people (Mark 6:4-6).

These verses recount the second time the townspeople of Nazareth rejected Jesus. The first time was in Luke 4 at the start of Jesus' ministry. On that visit, the people actually tried to kill Jesus. Nazareth was a tough place to visit.

The problem in Nazareth was a lack of honor. Dishonor towards Jesus was deeply embedded in the city. In Mark 6:4, Jesus said, "A prophet is honored everywhere except in his own hometown and among his relatives and his own family."

There is a connection between the lack of honor, unbelief, and the scarcity of miracles. If honor is not present, neither is belief, and when belief is not present, the miraculous works of God are limited. God's presence is attracted to honor. Verse 5 contains some chilling words: "and because of their unbelief He couldn't do any miracles among them." If we are contending for the miraculous of God, then we must choose to live with honor.

When we don't deal with our unrighteous judgments, we step into a trap of our own making and end up dishonoring God and people. In Nazareth the talk in the streets was something like this: "He's just Mary's son. Last week He fixed the door on my house. Who does He think He is?" And: "Hey, I know His brother. This guy is no Messiah. We went to school together!" God is always doing more in a life than we can see on the surface. Honor sees deeper.

The unbelief and dishonor in Nazareth was persistent. It was a pattern. Someone said once that if you do something once it is an accident. If you do it twice it is intentional. Nazareth was given over to dishonor, and the people had shut down the move of God in their midst.

We should ask ourselves some questions if we desire to walk in honor:

HOW DO WE HONOR SOMEONE WHO IS NOT HONORABLE?

Choose to prophesy to the gifts and destiny within that life. In the parable of the hidden treasure in the field, Jesus said the man wanted the treasure hidden in the field so badly that he bought the whole field, dirt and all, just to have the treasure. God is calling the Church to a level of radical love and honor so strong that we won't mind the dirt in someone's life as long as they became God's treasure in the end. When we honor another person, we are honoring a life assignment that came from eternity and was short-circuited in this realm. Giving honor jumps-starts a life and realigns a person with God's original intention for them.

HOW DO YOU HONOR SOMEONE WHO HAS FAILED YOU?

Speak the truth in love. Create a pathway of grace with your words so people can return from failure. Never compromise truth, and never use truth to beat someone into submission to your way of thinking. Truth spoken in love will set people free to become more. This freedom is part of what it means to honor someone. And the ones who give honor are set free from the need to punish the one who has wronged them.

If we choose to honor every person as a unique creation of God, then we will honor God. We will also experience the miraculous presence of God in our churches, our cities, and our nations that only honor can bring.

34
VISION CAST IN A CLOUD

For years I taught people how to create mission statements for themselves. It was a good idea, but I don't do that anymore.

At first these vision-planning sessions excited me. Then something changed. A hunger for something deeper began to move me away from what I had been doing. All of this vision casting became dry and laborious to me. I began to think, "Where was all of this programming and planning in the Word?" When I read the Scriptures, I find people who woke up everyday and had no idea what God had planned. They lived in a supernatural moment.

The more I looked into the Word, the more I saw people who had deep encounters with God, and those encounters became their vision. The Bible is filled with people like this. God revealed Himself to Paul on the Road to Damascus, and Paul left it all to follow Jesus. Peter stood in front of a fish BBQ on the shoreline after his denial and was restored. Jacob wrestled with God and then walked away with a limp and a new destiny. The church in Antioch was having a worship service when God told them to set apart Barnabas and Paul for a special assignment, and the Gentile mission was birthed. Elijah stood in the mouth of the cave, straining to hear the still voice of God, and then he heard Him. And then there was Moses the reluctant leader. Moses' anthem was, "God, can't you get somebody else?" God's encouragement to Moses was that His presence would go with him. He basically said, "Follow my presence Moses, and you'll get there." Moses ended up being one of the greatest leaders in Scripture.

God's presence is powerful. Presence defines who we are as the people of God. The only thing that distinguished the children of Israel from the surrounding nations was the presence of God. From a purely anthropological point of view, there was nothing different between Israel and the surrounding nations. The children of Israel had festivals and worshipped a deity like the other nations. The difference that defined them was the presence of the one true God in their midst. It hasn't changed since then. More than living a moral life, it is the presence of God in the Church that distinguishes us from the world around us. The Pharisees were moral, but they weren't led by God's presence.

In years past, some of us in church leadership have spent more time searching for vision in the business section of the local bookstore than seeking a life-changing encounter with God. We spent a lot of time honing the habits of highly effective people instead of living in a moment-by-moment hunger for His presence. Thankfully, many are parking that mentality in their past. Only out of His presence can a Spirit-inspired vision flow. Much of our "ministry" didn't require God to show up in order for it to get done—it just required a certain degree of busyness and planning.

There is a lot of burnout in the Church today because we can appear to be busy and still not be living moment by moment in His presence. In His presence is fullness of joy—nowhere else, not even in the midst of our perceived success.

In Exodus 19, a very insightful event takes place that reveals how God processed vision with Moses. In verse 9, the Lord said to Moses, "I am going to come to you in a dense cloud, so that the people will hear me speaking with you and will always put their trust in you." Some things in this verse can help us see how vision casting took place for Moses.

In verse 9, the Lord began by saying, "I will come to you. . . ." God is the One who comes to us with vision. We don't create vision and then invite Him to come to ours. Everything flows from Him. The beautiful part of this verse is that God is the One pursuing us with vision. In fact, He is the One who is always pursuing His people with vision.

In the Hebrew language, the word for "presence" can mean "face." When we choose to pursue the face of God in all areas of our lives, we invite His manifest presence to come. When we are in a season of doubt, the single most critical act we can do is to turn to God and seek His face. The direction and the answers we so desperately desire will take second place compared to the joy of simply seeking Him.

God said to Moses, "I will come to you in a thick cloud. . . ." This cloud was so dense that Moses could not see what was ahead of him. He was blinded. In order for God to birth vision in his people, He must first blind us to the sensory tools we normally rely upon. A thick cloud is not a place where you and I can really see anything. We are not in control in the cloud of His presence.

Are you in one of those moments when you can't see the next step? If you have given your heart to Him, chances are this is being done on purpose. He led you into the cloud of His presence. God has something He wants to show you, but He must first turn off your natural ability to process your circumstance. A season where you don't see anything sets you up to hear everything.

Then the Lord said to Moses, "I will come to you in a

thick cloud, Moses, so the people themselves can hear me when I speak with you. Then they will always trust you." Moses told the Lord what the people had said.

God said the people would hear Him speaking and would trust Moses' leadership. The most important thing someone can do to develop trust with those he or she serves is not to pursue success but to pursue God. God births trust in a leader when the people know a leader is in conversation with God.

The account of Moses on the mountain continued:

> On the morning of the third day, thunder roared and lightning flashed, and a dense cloud came down on the mountain. There was a long, loud blast from a ram's horn, and all the people trembled. Moses led them out from the camp to meet with God, and they stood at the foot of the mountain. All of Mount Sinai was covered with smoke because the Lord had descended on it in the form of fire. The smoke billowed into the sky like smoke from a brick kiln, and the whole mountain shook violently. As the blast of the ram's horn grew louder and louder, Moses spoke, and God thundered his reply. The Lord came down on the top of Mount Sinai and called Moses to the top of the mountain. So Moses climbed the mountain (Exodus 19:16-20).

This experience with God's presence did not happen just once. In Exodus 24, Moses spent forty days and forty nights on the mountain inside the cloud of glory. In Exodus 24:18, the text says, "Then Moses disappeared into the cloud." I think this is what a Kingdom vision is all about—the people of God disappearing into His presence so that only He is seen and heard. When people walk out of the cloud of His presence, they are changed forever.

35
SEEING JESUS IN A DIFFERENT FORM

I attended a very conservative Bible college that has changed for the better over the years. I can still remember buying a laminated Scripture reference note sheet that had one section titled, "Problem Scriptures." These problematic Scriptures were ones the author felt were not intended for the Church today. These "not-for-today" Scriptures had to do with healings, miracles, and the gifts of the Spirit.

Ten years after Bible college, after walking away from all things church, my wife and I had two children and felt it was time to reconnect with God. We began our search for a church where we were living, in the Willamette Valley of Oregon.

As a "not-for-today" person at the time, I found it odd that I found myself reacting negatively to church after church that preached a "not-for-today" message. The first three churches we visited went into great detail affirming that what happened in the Bible was somehow locked in the history of the Church and unattainable today because some professor in their Bible college said so.

I was fed up and disappointed with our search. I told Jan, "I am done looking for a church." With wisdom Jan said, "Can we try just one more?" I agreed and much to my horror she mentioned a church in Eugene, Oregon called Faith Center. I had heard some wild stories about that place.

On our arrival at Faith Center, I was immediately drawn to the honest passion the people had for God. I loved how they focused on Jesus and not all the foolish arguments about secondary issues I had been hearing for the past few weeks. We stayed, got touched by God, and were eventually sent out from Faith Center to plant our first church in Montana.

As the years have gone by, I have come to realize that Jesus appears in many different forms. Some of the ways He appears will actually violate our current understanding of Him. Most of our concepts of God are formed by our personal history and preferences and have little to do with a realistic picture of his life.

In Mark 16, Mark describes the incident where the disciples walked along the Road to Emmaus, sorrowfully discussing what had happened with Jesus. Verse 12 says, "Afterward he appeared in a different form. . . ." These disciples were only seeing Jesus in the past tense, so Jesus revealed himself in the present moment, and joy filled the disciples' hearts.

In verse 14, we see the disciples waiting behind closed doors in fear. To them, Jesus was dead and gone. Jesus then appeared to them in another form—in His resurrected body—and rebuked their unbelief. That time they were filled with joy and wonder as Jesus revealed himself in a different form.

In both cases, on the Road to Emmaus and behind doors in fear, Jesus had to appear in a different form in order to get the disciples' attention and to confront their disbelief. Jesus did this when He appeared to me in a different form at Faith Center and healed my broken life.

This issue has been a challenge in the Church for the last 2,000 years. Whenever Jesus comes in a form different from what is familiar to us, we can start talking like the new form can't be from God. We label it, "not for today" or "this is not of God." In the end, these ways of thinking can cause us to hunker down in our religious foxholes and focus our theological gun sights on anything that approaches our lives and challenges the status quo.

The early Church father, Augustine, is attributed with saying: "In essentials unity, in non-essentials liberty, and in all things love."

A danger in today's connected world is that people can appear like they know what they are talking about if they have Internet access and begin to parrot someone else's opinion. It must be true if it's on the Internet, right?

Most of these Internet and YouTube sparring matches are over what Augustine called the non-essentials. The non-essentials are things you don't go to hell over. These non-essentials are made up of our preferences and opinions, and they end up defining our closed circles of fellowship.

I remember the first pastors' conference I ever attended. I had been pastoring for a grand total of three weeks when I left my sweet wife and two kids in a new and unfamiliar town in Montana and drove by myself all the way to Portland, Oregon for the conference. I walked around the conference in an innocent and wide-eyed amazement at simply getting to be present and have someone call me "Pastor."

During one afternoon session, a very well-known pastor got up and shared a great word. As I took notes, I hoped that someday I could have about one-tenth of this man's wisdom. The next speaker got up, and I could tell he was not happy.

This second speaker went on to publicly disagree with the first pastor's position on the Second Coming of Christ— even before he began to preach on his given subject. I think the first man was a mid-Tribber and the correcting pastor was a staunch pre-Tribber. That was a hot-button issue in those days. I felt uncomfortable and wondered why this man was acting the way he did at this wonderful pastor-party. He was manifesting the "not-for-today" way of thinking that can attach itself to anything we disagree with.

That day at the pastor's conference I learned a valuable lesson:

THE SAME TRUTH CAN BE SEEN FROM TWO DIFFERENT ANGLES

My angle of Truth is not better than yours; it is simply different. We are both looking at the same beautiful object, and yet we are viewing it from different positions.

Years ago, a pastor who was new to our area and was going to take the leadership of a local church wanted to meet with me. My secretary made an appointment for us for the following week.

We met, introduced ourselves, and had a good conversation; we talked about our families, the beautiful Rogue Valley, and God. We talked for about an hour when, for some reason, the subject of women in ministry came up. I voiced how excited I was to see women released to do whatever God asked of them and how I enjoyed their perspective as they taught the Word of God.

It was like someone had changed the atmospheric pressure in the room. This smiling-faced pastor went stern. From his leaning-back-on-the-couch posture he leaned forward and said, "Having a woman teach a man is in the same league as saying that salvation can be had apart from Jesus."

I was stunned. I had to ask him to repeat what he said. He repeated it, but this time around he provided even more emphasis. I felt gut-punched. Our conversation stumbled on for a few more minutes, and then we parted ways. I never saw him again. He is no longer pastoring the church he came to lead. I wish him well wherever he is and hope he is seeing from a different perspective.

That day in my office, I learned another valuable lesson:

WHAT WE THINK WE KNOW ABSOLUTELY IS NOT ALWAYS ABSOLUTE

That dear brother had narrowed God down to such a small field of focus that if Jesus ever dared to show up expressing anything feminine, the man would have labeled it as "of the devil."

When Jesus gave us the Great Commission, He wasn't giving us the fine points of our personally interpreted views of theology. He was giving us the essentials of the faith that need to remain intact in order for us to be considered the Church. These essentials are found most clearly in the simple and profound creeds of the Church. There are not as many of these essentials as some people think.

In all the years I have been following Jesus, I have come to realize there are a lot of non-essentials. We need to give each other some slack with these, or they can kill our agape love and show the world that the Church is not really worth investigating. Jesus didn't get into the non-essentials. He left those with us to struggle together in love in order to find some common ground. This is where humility plays such a huge role in the health and vitality of the Church.

Jesus has always been in the business of showing up in another form than we are familiar with, and—in His arrival—confronting our unbelief. As I mentally scrolled through the Scriptures I saw Jesus do this a lot.

He appeared:

- As the Creator at the creation
- As the great I Am who spoke to Moses from a burning bush
- As the rock that gushed forth living water in the

wilderness
- As a baby in a manger
- As a twelve-year-old boy in the Temple going about His Father's business
- As a carpenter's Son in His unbelieving hometown of Nazareth
- As the first prophet of a New Covenant
- As a drunk and demon-possessed cult-leader to the Pharisees
- As a teacher to those who wanted to learn
- As a problematic revolutionary to the Roman government
- As a healer to the diseased
- As an impotent, false prophet hanging on a criminal's cross to those who convicted Him
- As a brother to his brothers
- As a Son to His Father
- As a miracle baby to His mother
- As the resurrected Lord to those who arrived at the tomb

How Jesus appears to us and our response to Him will depend on the condition of our hearts. How we perceive those who come in His name will also depend on the condition of our hearts. Jesus may look very different in each of His manifestations, but he will always be the same yesterday, today, and forever. He is both the same and different. This is why we have to be careful if we ever find ourselves saying "not for today" or "this can't be of God" because the lesser images of God we have created by our non-essentials thinking may be the very things He is coming to heal.

36
THE NEXT BIG THING

As a pastor, I receive some of the latest information about what is taking place within the Church world. A lot of what I read is the search for "The Next Big Thing" coming to the Church.

Over the years, I have seen this search take people on a quest for larger churches, the latest in staff structures, new ways to preach to disinterested people, and the list goes on and on. This never-ending search for "The Next Big Thing" is a journey that can lead to frustration, performance, and compromise.

I have come to realize that the only "Next Big Thing" I care to invest my life in is a new and fresh move of God's Spirit where the unexplainable and immeasurable works of God take place and where lives are changed.

When I am in pursuit of "The Next Big Thing," I leave in my wake a disconnection from the only thing that really matters—His presence. Out of His presence flows all that is valuable and worthy. The early disciples sought His presence in worship in Acts 13, and from that gathering the mission to the entire Gentile world was birthed, and that experience with His presence is still being felt today.

At this point in my journey, I am giving God permission to recalibrate the direction of my life and all that I pursue in His name. I believe that many of us with this similar passion will see God begin to do "The Next Big Thing" in our midst, but His presence has always been "The Only Thing."

37

WHEN WE USED TO WEAR SUITS

When I started in full-time ministry many years ago, most of us wore jackets and ties to preach on Sunday morning. Recently, I looked at some old pictures of me back in the early 1980's, and according to the fashion standards of the day I looked just fine. Today, those pictures are embarrassing.

A change took place somewhere in the late 80's when the brave among us decided to ditch the coat and tie and replace it with an open collar, sweater, and slacks. This went on for a few years until someone decided to wear jeans. We all wanted to wear jeans but needed someone to grant us "permission" to do it.

I remember the first time I wore jeans. It was for a Wednesday evening service. I felt both naked and free. I got some comments. I was surprised that most of the people thought it was cool. We began to discover that jeans actually worked, and a few years later, they began to show up behind many Sunday morning pulpits. Today, I can only remember a few Sundays in the last ten years when I have not worn a pair of jeans to preach.

The nice thing about jeans is that you can dress them up or down. Most Sundays I wear a nice shirt with my jeans. On those occasions where I want to dress it up a bit, I choose a dark sport coat over an un-tucked shirt.

I still have what I call a "marrying and burying" suit hanging in my closet. This nice black suit comes out a few times each year to help a young couple begin their journey of life together or to conduct a funeral for someone who passed into the presence of the Lord. I wore my black suit just last week to conduct a marriage ceremony. It actually felt good and brought back some memories.

I mention all of this about attire to process a simple point. The packaging of ministry has changed over the years and will continue to do so for many years to come. It's OK to change things, in fact I think it's a sign of health. The Church is one group that can actually get stuck in time and call it righteousness.

If Jesus were to show up today and manifest in a physical body, He would not be wearing a robe or sandals. He would be dressed like the rest of us. Sometimes we make Jesus too mysterious. The Incarnation—Jesus taking on a physical body like ours—was His idea. He wanted to first fit in so He could stand out. Jesus was good at removing barriers to communication.

When Jesus went to His hometown of Nazareth, He dressed like the audience to whom He spoke. When He finished speaking, they decided that He was just too familiar to them to be the real Messiah, so they tried to kill Him by attempting to throw Him over a cliff. Looking contemporary has a downside.

While I think Jesus' attire would change with the times, I know His message never changes.

When Jesus stood in the synagogue in Nazareth and was handed the scroll, He read from Isaiah 61. As He read these words He was dressed in the garb of His day:

The Spirit of the Sovereign Lord is upon me, for the Lord has anointed me to bring good news to the poor. He has sent me to comfort the brokenhearted and to proclaim that captives will be released and prisoners will be freed. He has sent me to tell those who mourn that the time of the Lord's favor has come, and with it, the day of God's anger against their enemies. To all who mourn in Israel, he will give a crown of beauty for ashes, a joyous blessing instead of mourning, festive praise instead of despair. In their righteousness, they will be like great oaks that the Lord has planted for his own glory (vs. 1-3).

Over all the years that I have done the stuff of ministry, I have tried to keep the message of the Gospel intact while cultural change was taking place all around me. The way we dress and what we drive will adjust as new products are marketed our way and we agree with those changes by exercising our choice as consumers. What will hopefully not change is the message of Jesus found in Isaiah 61. You can speak these words dressed in anything and deliver them at anytime and they will always bring life.

38
THE JESUS-MIRACLE MODEL OF EVANGELISM

Our primary model for how to do anything is Jesus. He is our example for how to love. He is our model for leadership. And He is our method of evangelism. Whenever you need to find a way to do anything, look at Jesus first, and find out how He did it.

I enjoy reading Mark's gospel account. The Gospel of Mark is a compressed revelation of how Jesus ministered. When I need a quick infusion of the bare essentials of Jesus' life and ministry, I find myself reading Mark. His writing is like a refreshing swim on a hot day.

In the first chapter of Mark, the people of Capernaum were listening to Jesus teach in the synagogue on the Sabbath. Verse 22 says, "The people were amazed at his teaching, for he taught with real authority—quite unlike the teachers of religious law."

The people of Capernaum came to this conclusion because they saw the difference between a teacher who simply shares facts (a Pharisee) and Jesus who shared revelatory truth from the Father. The difference between these two forms of teaching is vast. Jesus revealed to His listeners what the Father had just revealed to Him in the moment: it was fresh revelation that brought freedom. The Pharisees, on the other hand, shared facts about the past and placed impossible burdens on people.

In verse 23, a demon-possessed man suddenly appeared in the synagogue and began shouting. Jesus cut the demon short and said, "Be quiet! Come out of the man" (vs. 25). With those words, the evil spirit screamed, threw the man into a convulsion, and came out. You can almost sense the shocked quiet and stillness in the synagogue in those moments immediately following this man's deliverance as people were asking themselves the question, "What just happened?"

The break in the silence came in verse 27 with the people asking, "'What sort of new teaching is this? they asked excitedly.' It has such authority!" The news of this event launched out from the synagogue and began to spread throughout the entire region of Galilee.

What caught my attention was verse 22. There, we are told the people were amazed at His teaching. This amazement could be interpreted through the lens of our Western concept of academic authority. In our contemporary culture, good teaching is seen as the result of diligent study and preparation of factual data presented within a logical development and delivered in an engaging form of communication. You could come to that conclusion if verse 22 was pulled out of context.

However, moments after the demon-possessed man was set free by the command of Jesus, comes the fuller understanding of how the people that day understood "teaching with authority." The question in verse 27 reveals the answer for us, "'What sort of new teaching is this?' they asked excitedly. It has such authority. Even evil spirits obey his orders!"

For the people in the synagogue, real authority in teaching was linked to the demonstration of what was being taught. It was in the demonstration of God's truth that the authority of Christ was released to do what would be impossible to accomplish without God's power.

As soon as the deliverance of the demon-possessed man took place, "The news about Jesus spread quickly throughout the entire region of Galilee" (vs. 28). As this news circulated, the testimony functioned like a net, gathering the sick and demon-possessed of that region and bringing them to Jesus:

> That evening after sunset, many sick and demon-possessed people were brought to Jesus. The whole town gathered at the door to watch (Mark 1:32-33).

Embedded in this verse is a concept for evangelism that applies to the Church today. The only way that entire cities—"the whole town"—will show up is when Jesus is allowed to teach and demonstrate His truth through us. The Gospel message includes a release of supernatural activity in the form of signs, wonders, and miracles. Our cities will not show up at our doorstep if we are teaching well-crafted messages alone without the actual demonstration of what was taught.

People have always come to see what God was doing. On the Day of Pentecost, the people of the city of Jerusalem came to that outpouring to see what was taking place. Acts 2:6 tells us, "When they heard the loud noise, everyone came running. . . . "

I think the Church today is rediscovering how to love and serve our cities. We need to get out of our church buildings and engage our communities with God's love.

People don't usually come running to see something the Church is doing that a service club can accomplish without God's help. Acts of kindness are wonderful, but they are not the only thing that happened in the Gospel accounts. The people in the Gospel of Mark came running to see something that could never be accomplished by the best of our good works. They came running because they heard that Jesus was healing the sick and setting the demon-possessed free. They came running to see the Kingdom of God taking place on earth.

After he healed the demon-possessed man, Jesus healed a man with leprosy:

> [T]he man went and spread the word, proclaiming to everyone what had happened. As a result, large crowds soon surrounded Jesus, and he couldn't publicly enter a town anywhere. He had to stay out in the secluded places, but people from everywhere kept coming to him (Mark 1:45).

The healed man, and the testimony about his miracle, spread throughout the area, announcing that Jesus was in town.

When Jesus told us in the Great Commission of Matthew 28 to go and make disciples, He said those words right after the sentence in verse 18 where He declared, "'I have been given all authority in heaven and on earth.'"

Right after the events of Mark 1, chapter 2 begins with four men tearing apart the roof of a house and lowering a paralyzed friend through the opening into a crowded living room where Jesus was waiting. The first words out of Jesus' mouth were: "My child, your sins are forgiven" (Mark 2:5). The teachers of religious law got upset with Jesus and questioned His authority to forgive sins. Jesus went on to say:

> "So, I will prove to you that the Son of Man has the authority on earth to forgive sins." Then Jesus turned to the paralyzed man and said, "Stand up, pick up your mat, and go home" (vs. 10-11).

It was a dramatic miracle in front of stunned onlookers.

As I read this account, I saw the obvious linkage between healing and evangelism. The forgiving of the paralyzed man's sins, and his subsequent healing, would dramatically change the environment of the entire region.

Healing linked to evangelism was a reoccurring theme in Jesus' ministry. The majority of the people in our communities will only be reached when something supernatural begins to interrupt the flow of their naturally limited lives. Good works alone can never do this.

The room that day was crowded, not because a good teacher was conducting a Bible Study. The room was crowded because Jesus had been healing people.

Jesus' authority came into operation for purposes beyond teaching a memorable message. This is the same authority that demanded a demon to come out of a possessed man and healed the leper. It is the same authority that forgave sin and healed a paralyzed man, allowing him to jump up, pick up his mat, and walk back home through the stunned crowd who had gathered to see the demonstration of Christ's authority.

While the Church rediscovers the joy of going out and doing acts of love in our communities, it is important to remember that people will come running to see something supernatural taking place in their midst. Our acts of service are intended to be acts of love and a means to bring us into contact with broken people who might need a miracle. Miracles are what Jesus used to evangelize the world in His day, and they are what God wants to use to expand His Kingdom in our world today.

39
RESTOCKING THE SHELVES OF MINISTRY

Leslie Keegel, the President of the Foursquare churches in Sri Lanka, spoke in our church in Medford, Oregon. Leslie leads 1,500 churches in his home nation. He carries an apostolic anointing along with a strong gift of revelation and miraculous healing. Throughout the three days Leslie was with us, he shared in various venues: in our public services, in a gathering of regional pastors and leaders, and in our school of ministry. In each setting, something of the supernatural heart of God was deposited in our lives.

Leslie prophesied about the destiny of our local church. In his prophecy, was both a promise and a responsibility. Leslie said Living Waters Church would become a wellspring of miraculous healing to this region and to the nation. That was our promise.

Leslie also said that God was asking us to be intentional as we pursue the supernatural and to be willing to take risks in faith. We were told to deal with any reluctance and reticence that would hold us back in a place of comfort. That was our responsibility.

Whenever a leader ministers, I watch and learn. I watch for the pauses that tell me he or she is listening for something fresh from God. I watch to see if someone is drawing from a dated bag of proven ministry formulas and principles that lack fresh revelation. I watch to discern the source of what is being ministered.

As I watched Leslie, I saw a man who extended his hand into eternity, through the veil that separates what is seen and unseen, and who waited for God to place words in his hand to bring back into this realm. Leslie reached out in faith and brought back something supernatural from God. This is how miracles happen.

After I dropped Leslie off at the airport, I was alone to process what God had spoken through this anointed servant of God. I went to sleep that night pondering the future. During the night I had a dream. In the dream I saw an old basement storage room lined with wooden shelves. The shelves were partially filled with old canned goods. Everything was covered in dust, and the storeroom looked neglected. The air was stale and still.

When I awoke the next morning, I sought the Lord for a meaning of the dream. I began to hear the Lord say that many of us who lead the church need to restock the storehouse of our hearts. Many of us have been ministering with cans that have expired labels. Instead of reaching into eternity for something fresh, we are reaching into a dusty and dated storeroom. These shelves can only be restocked with day-by-day, fresh encounters with God. These new and fresh words from God are retrieved because we have reached into His presence in faith.

I am praying this prayer for myself: "Father, today I choose to reach into your presence and wait until you drop something into my hand. When I sense the weight of your word in my hand, I will bring that miraculous word back into this realm, expecting to see things happen that are beyond all that I would dare to ask or think."

40

GOD'S HOUR GLASS

I was asked to speak at a men's retreat in Central Oregon. The Sunday before I left, on my way out of the sanctuary, one of the women in our church stopped me and said, "Garris, I believe I have a word for you about the men's retreat: you are to go unprepared." I thanked this faithful woman for sharing the word with me and I went home.

Later that day, I realized what "going unprepared" meant for me. This meant that while I would go unprepared in a traditional sense, I would not go without a word from the Lord.

Sure enough, in prayer over the next few days, the Lord gave me an image that would become the word for these men. I share this image now because its truth touches all of us. The image was of one of those old hourglasses that measured time by draining sand from the upper compartment to the lower. In the image I saw, the last few grains of sand were trickling downward, and the hourglass was about to run out of time.

As I looked at the hourglass, I saw the hand of God

enter the image, pick up the hourglass, and turn it over. Then the Lord said, "Tell the men that some of them feel like their time has run out, but I am about to change that. I am turning over their hour glass and giving them a new season."

As I thought of this word, I grabbed it for myself. Never before, with all the cultural change and financial crisis going on, have I felt like time, as we know it, is running out. For days I kept seeing that image whenever a faithless lie would try to rear its ugly head and attempt to deprive me of hope. I kept seeing the hand of God come into the scene and change everything.

God is reaching into our lives; His hand is picking up our hourglass and turning it over. I believe the Church is entering a new season when we will see the hand of God do this very thing on both a personal and corporate level.

There was one final word the Lord spoke concerning this image as I made my way through the mountains of Central Oregon to the retreat. He said for me to tell the men, "You have another season—I am not done with you yet!"

That is a good word for all of us.

41

THE PIVOT POINT

I have been talking to believers about establishing their "pivot point." A pivot point is that place where you conceptually put one of your feet and say, "This is my bottom line. I can't give this up." Not a lot should occupy that spot.

A pivot point is a good way to visualize the Augustine quote I mentioned before: "In essentials unity, in non-essentials liberty, and in all things love." Augustine was wise. He knew that as the Church developed, some people would start to get nervous if other believers did not live their faith in lock-step agreement with them.

I have always thought the essentials should be reserved for those things that had to do with God and with Jesus who said, "I am the way, the truth, and the life. No one can come to the Father except through me" (John 14:6). I want my feet firmly planted in those essentials because without them we don't have a biblical Christianity.

The power of having a pivot point is that I can pivot towards something new without disconnecting with the essentials and closing the door on an expanding circle of fellowship. I can pivot towards the Presbyterians and bring something Presbyterian back into my pivot point. I can pivot towards a healing revival and bring back a new level of faith from a revivalist. I can pivot towards a Catholic and bring back a new respect and reverence for Communion. As we pivot, with our belief in the essentials firm and unshakeable, spending time with different kinds of Christians is actually a lot of fun.

42

THE FIFTY-YEAR LETTER

About twenty years ago, I changed how I counsel couples who come to me wanting to get married. I used to struggle with why I didn't like the more traditional approach of having couples read books and take tests to direct their new relationship. That approach just didn't fit with me, though I invite other leaders to do marital counseling using those resources if they work for them.

The change came as a word from the Lord to me: "Have the couples write a letter about what they want this relationship to become in fifty years, and I will give them the desires of their hearts."

Right after that word, a couple came in for premarital marriage counseling, and I shared with them how the Lord had changed my approach to our time together. At the end of our first meeting, I asked the couple to craft a single-page letter about what they desired to take place in their marriage in the coming fifty years. I asked them to bring the completed letter to our next meeting.

The next time we met, I asked to see their letter and

quietly read it to myself as the couple waited. Like all couples in love, they were holding hands and making eyes at each other. After I read the letter, we talked about the ceremony, and then I asked them to schedule three more appointments with me.

When this young couple left my office, I reread the letter and highlighted the areas they wrote about: love, communication, family, finances, dreams, ministry, and so on. Over the next few months, as we met together, I unpacked each of their desires and added personal and biblical insight to them. The couple eventually got married and began to live out what was written in their Fifty-Year Letter.

The assignment I gave to this couple, and to many more like them over the years, was to keep this letter in a safe place and bring it out each anniversary and read it aloud together. When they finish reading it each year, they are to ask each other how they are doing in their relationship in comparison to the desires expressed in their letter. Each year, the letter becomes an annual marriage tune-up—or a call for a major overhaul, if needed.

God enjoys giving us the desires of our hearts. There is, however, a condition in His giving us our desires: we must first delight ourselves in Him. Delighting in the Lord means that His values become our values. What makes Him happy makes us happy and so on.

Psalm 37:4 tells us, "Take delight in the Lord, and he will give you your heart's desires." The delighting in God precedes his giving us the desires of our heart.

When I meet a young couple to counsel them for the first time, before I give them their writing assignment, I share how God feels about marriage and how much He wants their marriage to succeed. It is from the desire of God's heart towards them that a delight in Him emerges. A God-directed passion and a delighting in God together is where growth as a couple takes place. This is why I believe

God changed how I counsel couples wanting to get married.

In my office file cabinet is a section filled with Fifty-Year Letters written by many couples. From time to time, I take out the letters and pray for the couples. I pray that the passion they had for each other in the beginning, and the delight they shared together in the Lord in my office, would still be burning stronger than ever with each passing anniversary.

43

THE GREAT OMISSION

When Jesus gave us the Great Commission he said, "'go and make disciples of all the nations'" (Matthew 28:19). The Great Commission has become the marching orders for the Church.

Toward the end of Mark's Gospel, Jesus told his disciples to "go" in another way. He said, "'Go into all the world and preach the Good News to everyone'" (Mark 16:15). Two verses later, he said, "'These miraculous signs will accompany those who believe'" (vs. 17a). When he uttered these words, Jesus made it clear that the preaching of the Gospel would forever be connected with supernatural ministry.

We have the Great Commission well defined. We understand much of what Jesus was telling his disciples in Matthew 28. In fact, there is a significant industry within the Church relating to this aspect of our calling. You can buy books on the subject, read doctoral dissertations on discipleship, and even attend conferences where we are told how to do the Great Commission by some of the brightest minds in the Church. With all of this availability on the subject of discipleship, not much of what we are doing is impacting our American culture.

What we don't have down is the "go" part defined by Jesus in Mark 16: "'These miraculous signs will accompany those who believe.'" Many in the Church are comfortable with the Great Commission of Matthew 28 but get nervous with the signs, wonders, and miracles aspect of our commission.

The commissioning of the Church in Mark 16 has become, even within some historic Pentecostal and Charismatic groups, the Great Omission. The dictionary defines an omission as something we neglect. Miracles, signs, and wonders were used by Jesus to get the attention of His culture so He could tell them about the Kingdom of God. Jesus did not neglect anything. He used it all to glorify the Father.

The very thing that will get the attention of our unbelieving culture—the supernatural—has many times been omitted from the message we are trying to preach. We would never actually come out and say this, but there is very little supernatural evidence accompanying the vast majority of what we do within the American Church. I frequently have to ask myself, "What am I doing that requires God to show up in power?"

Our cities and our nations are waiting to experience what I would call, "The Greater Commission." The Greater Commission melds together the commission Jesus gave us in Matthew 28 and Mark 16 to become a disciple-making people who walk in the miraculous power of Christ before the cultures of the world. There is not a culture on earth that can withstand the powerful combination found in The Greater Commission.

44
EXCHANGING THE NOW FOR THE NEW

Recently, on my morning commute, I turned on my car's CD player and a worship song began to declare words about taking us where we've never been and where we're scared to go. Those words touched me, and I found myself pressing the replay button again and again, letting the words sink deeper into my heart.

The "never been" places in our lives are those new places where we might be afraid to go because they are unfamiliar, untested, and unknown. The fear that can surround our future is the very place into which God invites us to step as we learn to trust Him at new and deeper levels.

Later in the day of that commute, I was sharing with our pastoral staff the long-term, ministry-transition plan the Lord has revealed for Jan and me. The plan was actually given to us before we arrived in Medford, Oregon. For the last several years, we have been walking out the plan privately in our hearts. Making the plan visible and verbal today is causing a whole host of emotions to rise up within me.

Our transition will require a few years to fully accomplish, but it will take a visible step forward once shared. This is the beginning of the closure of over three decades of doing ministry in a known and familiar pastoral assignment. With every closure, there is always an opening if we are willing to look by faith into our future. Moving into the new requires that we let go of the now. We need faith to do this. If we are willing to let go, we will have the empty hands required to receive the new season God has been preparing for us.

As Jan and I reach out in faith and begin walking towards our new future, we will be taking hold of something that will feel as new as it did many years ago when we took hold of our first ministry assignment. With God, each season is new.

45

THE MYTH OF HEROES AND SUCCESS

Twenty years ago, I sat in a large convention center with several thousand pastors. We were attending a denominational conference. One of the scheduled speakers had to cancel at the last moment, and Roger Whitlow, a pastor of a large and impacting church in Fresno, California, was asked to speak in his place.

The Valley Christian Center in Fresno had grown over the years to thousands of people. The church had a beautiful facility and school. Its ministry impacted a city and a region. I heard Roger speak on several occasions, and he is one of the most solid and balanced leaders I had ever listened to. I still have some of his notes from when I was a student and the contents ring as true today as they did decades ago.

To the best of my memory, when Roger stepped up to speak, these were some of the first words out of his mouth:

> Many of you think what is taking place in Fresno is because I am some great leader. You see the numbers of people coming to our church and think its all happening because of me. Let me tell you the truth. God decided to

do something special in Fresno, and I just happened to be the pastor leading the church when all of this happened. It wasn't because of me. It was because God decided to do this on my watch.

When Roger finished speaking there was a pause. The atmosphere of the meeting began to shift. Something strange took place—I could sense a collective sigh of relief sweep across the room. I was one of those sighing. Something was being broken off.

At the time of this conference, pastors in the American Church were in the midst of a season when we were being asked to attend conferences with titles like, "Breaking the 200 Barrier." Numerical markers were being laid down to denote ministerial success. Your emotions and self-worth were determined on which side of the numerical barrier you found yourself.

A subtle message was being sent out via the large glossy conference invitations that came to our church mailboxes inferring that only beyond certain numbers could we really be doing something significant for God. It didn't help that denominations across the nation supported this error of thinking by "platforming" pastors of larger ministries as a way to encourage us to "break out." It didn't work. It just got a lot of us depressed in the process of comparison.

As Roger Whitlow's words of freedom were released, the weighted yoke of having to produce something defined as numerical "success" began to lift off many of the leaders present that day. What was being broken off was the yoke of the lie that says, "Bigger is Always Better."

Today, many of the leaders I talk to within the Church are waiting for something to happen. The danger in times like these is to respond in the way we did twenty years ago. What we really need today, like we did twenty years ago, is an encounter with God. We really don't need another conference or the acquisition of a new skill set.

Most of us have attended the conferences, enrolled in

the self-analysis programs or even added a fresh skill set in an attempt to do old things in a new way. These attempts have failed as a jump-start. They fail because they try to do what only God can do.

Anymore, when I pray for people, I only pray for an encounter with God. I pray for one of those supernatural Book of Acts kind of encounters that so radically shifts the life of a pastor that the culture of the church they lead is also shifted. When the Church discovers God in a fresh way, the culture will also share in the shift. This is the domino effect of a God-encounter.

Over the years, I keep hearing the words of Roger Whitlow. They make more sense today than when I first heard them twenty years ago. Roger reminded us that we don't need another leader at a conference who makes us think that anything other than a God-encounter will make a difference in the long run. He reminded us that what we need is for God to show up.

46
RE-COMMISSIONED LIVES

As I looked out from my hotel room in Long Beach, I saw the great Queen Mary passenger ship docked across the harbor. She was visible through an urban forest of yacht masts, man-planted palm trees, and a large dock cranes. In the distance, freighters inched across the horizon past offshore oil platforms.

From the seventh-floor window of my hotel, the Queen Mary captured my thoughts. She is big, all 1,130 feet of her. She looks like a 1930's movie image. In my mind, I could see the old movie reel depicting the walkway leading up to the ship and the men and women dressed in formal attire waving from the ship's deck to their friends below.

This iconic ship was the flagship of the Cunard Line from 1936 to 1967. Early in her life she worked as a troop ship during World War II. She transported royalty and heads of state for three decades. Her résumé was one of the most impressive in maritime history.

Today, she rests at a permanent dock within the Long Beach Harbor as a hotel and museum. Her great engines are silent. No foaming wake follows her from port to port. Now, only small waves lap against her sides from within a protected harbor. The only reason the Queen Mary sits today in the Long Beach Harbor is because the City of Long Beach out-bid Japanese scrap metal companies who would have reduced her to a pile of recycled metal.

I began to process what it might feel like to be decommissioned like the Queen Mary. Lately, I have been meeting people who are going through major changes in their lives, so the subject has been on my mind. People see their career-ending dock coming, and they don't know what to do with the change and transition.

Never did the designers of the Queen Mary envision their majestic creation ending up in a permanent dock as a tourist attraction. A purist designer might not have signed on to the project had he known of the eventual fate of his plan.

I think God, in His mercy, keeps us ignorant of some aspects of our future because He has not yet released the measure of grace required to handle the eventual dispositions of some seasons of our lives.

Later, on my flight home from Long Beach, I sat next to a man in his mid-fifties who was just laid off unexpectedly from his job. He didn't know what to do. He was sitting at a personal dock with no place to go. I don't think my new-found friend ever imagined that at age fifty-five he would be out of work and wondering what to do next. He felt decommissioned.

Before I left Long Beach, I walked across the harbor bridge to see the Queen Mary up close and personal. As my walk brought me closer to this great ship, my thoughts began to orbit around the word "purpose." This ship, as grand as she was and is, was created for a single purpose— to carry people from one port to another. That purpose is transferrable. Real, God-breathed purpose is always transferrable because it comes from eternity and is never limited by the varied and unpredictable seasons of life. That transferrable purpose is what I used to encourage my new, out-of-work friend later that day as our flight droned through the night back to Oregon.

As I stood on the dock looking up at the Queen Mary, she gave me the impression of a mounted trophy head of an African game animal hanging on a paneled den wall. You looked up, waiting for the head to move, but it was forever frozen in a taxidermist-created stare. You know that the animal would look a lot better back in the wild doing what God had created it to do instead of being a wall ornament. Our lives were never meant to be docked or mounted. Life moves on.

The time for the Queen Mary, in her present form, was over. Travel needs have changed since she was first designed. New cruise line concepts have been developed. The past had to be docked to build something new for future passages.

However, the core purpose of the Queen Mary was not lost because she was decommissioned. Her purpose, to carry passengers, was transferred into other vessels. When the Queen Mary went to dock in Long Beach, passenger travel on the oceans didn't stop. It continued on in new designs for other ships. The marine designers didn't stop creating new vessels at the decommissioning of the Queen Mary. God is not about to stop redesigning the lives of those who carry His purpose. He always has a new design waiting to be discovered.

The wise ones will not stare at their docked life, but they will take their purpose in life back to the drawing boards and ask the heavenly Master Builder what kind of new vessel He has planned for the next season of their lives. God wants to break our focus from a docked life, and the numbing sorrow at what was, and get us excited about what is to come.

Shipbuilders of today design ships on computer screens;

their designs will be wrapped around the purpose of a vessel. Designs change, purpose does not. The ship of your future is already floating in the heart of God.

The purpose of God in your life is never docked, only the vessel that carried the purpose is, and that docking is only done to make way for a new vessel to carry His purpose into new ports of call. God desires to re-commission our lives for new seasons of service.

Garris Elkins

Ministry website:

www.garriselkins.com

Ministry address:

Garris Elkins
Prophetic Horizons
P.O. Box 509
Jacksonville, Oregon
97530

23132712R00085

Made in the USA
Charleston, SC
12 October 2013